Best Monologues

For ALL Auditions

(And How To Prepare For Them!)

Best Monologues For ALL Auditions

(And How To Prepare For Them!)

Glenn Alterman

A Smith and Kraus Book

A Smith and Kraus Book
177 Lyme Road, Hanover, NH 03755
editorial 603.643.6431 To Order 1.877.668.8680
www.smithandkraus.com

Best Monologues for All Auditions
(And How to Prepare for Them!)
Copyright © 2018 by Glenn Alterman
All rights reserved.

Manufactured in the United States of America

CAUTION: Professionals and amateurs are hereby warned that the material represented in this book is subject to a royalty. It is fully protected under the copyright laws of the United States of America, and of all countries covered by the International Copyright Union (including the Dominion of Canada and the rest of the British Commonwealth), and of all countries covered by the Pan-American Copyright Convention and the Universal Copyright Convention, and of all countries with which the United States has reciprocal copyright relations. All rights, including professional, amateur, motion picture, recitation, lecturing, public reading, radio broadcasting, television, video or sound taping, all other forms of mechanical or electronic reproductions such as information storage and retrieval systems and photocopying, and the rights of translation into foreign languages, are strictly reserved.

ISBN: 9781575259185
Library of Congress Control Number: 2017958535

Typesetting and layout by Elizabeth E. Monteleone
Cover by Olivia Monteleone
Author photo by Robert Kim

For information about custom editions, special sales, education and corporate purchases, please contact Smith and Kraus at editor@smithandkraus.com or 603.643.6431.

Acknowledgements

The author wishes to thank the following theater companies for their help in developing all the monologues in this book. Each of the monologues received multiple readings by actors in these companies for feedback and timing.

New Circle Theater Company
American Renaissance Theater Company
The Workshop Theater Company
The Miramax Playwrights Group

TABLE OF CONTENTS

Introduction 17

CHAPTER 1

All About Monologues And Auditions 19
    What Is A Monologue?
    Why Actors Need Monologues
    Types of Monologue Auditions
    When You Finally Get The Agent Office Interview
    The Casting Director Interview
    The Theater Company General Audition
    E.P.A.'s (Equity Principal Auditions)
    Monologue Auditions For Film
    Monologues For Classroom Work

CHAPTER 2

Marketing Yourself With The "Right" Monologue 25

CHAPTER 3

Rehearsing The Monologue 29

CHAPTER 4

Casting Directors Advice For Monologue Auditions 33
    Insights From Casting Directors James Calleri, Alan
    Filderman, Diane Heery, Arnold Mungioli, Breanna

Benjamin, Sandra Steiner, Adrienne Stern, Robert Longston
Casting Directors On The Most Common Monologue Mistakes Actors Make at Monologue Auditions
Casting Director James Calleri, Alan Filderman, Diane Heery, Arnold Mungioli, Breanna Benjamin, Sandra Steiner, Adrienne Stern
Mistakes Actors Make At Monologue Auditions
Casting Director Risa Bramon Garcia On Monologue Auditions and Advice For ALL Auditions

CHAPTER 5

Monologue Guide For the Monologues In This Book   43

WOMEN'S MONOLOGUES

MARLA   47
    (Dramatic) (40's to 60's) All venues (1 minute 22 seconds)
    (After being in a serious car accident with her husband, Marla vents her feelings to him)

MARY   48
    (Dramatic) (20's to 40's) All venues (1 minute 22 seconds)
    (Mary yearns to connect with a man she sees across the dance floor. An inner monologue)

HELENA   49
    (Serio-comedic) (30's to 40's) All venues (1 minute 13 seconds)
    (Helena sets up a date with a man to meet at a motel)

TERRY   50
    (From AFTER by Glenn Alterman)
    (Comedy) (Middle aged) All venues (1 minute)
    (Terry tells a man she just met why she loves going to funerals)

CYNDI 51
>   (Dramatic) (30's to late 40's) Agent's office, auditions with longer audition time (2 minute 12 seconds)
>   (Cyndi recalls the night she tried to take Manny home from a bar)

MONICA 54
>   (Comedic) (20's to 30's) All venues (1 minute)
>   (Monica tells off her close girlfriend after finding out some upsetting news)

SHERRY 55
>   (Comedic) (20's to 30's) Agent's office, auditions allowing a longer audition time (2 minutes 25 seconds)
>   (Sherry enjoys meeting men at bars and going off with them, ending each night with a big surprise)

CHERYL 57
>   (Dramatic) (20's to 30's) All venues (1 minute 15 seconds)
>   (Cheryl recalls seeing a moment like the present one, growing up. An inner monologue)

GINGER 58
>   (Serio-comedic) (Teenager) Agent's office, longer audition time (1 minute 58 seconds)
>   (Ginger has a life-threatening incident occur while she's looking at a boy she likes)

HELENE 60
>   (Serio-comedic) (Mid 20's to early 40's) Agent's office, auditions with longer audition time (2 minutes 25 seconds)
>   (Helene recalls a terrifying incident that happened on the way to meet her fiancés parents)

TELLY 62
>   (From BENCHMARKS by Glenn Alterman)
>   (Comedic) (Adult any age)
>   All venues (1 minute 20 seconds)
>   (A woman waiting for a bus at a bus stop starts talking to a stranger)

SHE 63
    (From THE KINDNESS OF ENEMIES by Glenn Alterman)
    (Comedic) (Adult-any age) All venues (1 minute)
    (After going home with a man she met at a bar, SHE tells him what she hopes will happen next in their relationship)

JACKI 64
    (From PHONE by Glenn Alterman)
    (Serio-comedic) (20's-30's) All venues (1 minute 53 seconds)
    (Jacki talks about why she's in a toxic relationship with the man she's with)

BETTE 66
    (Comedy) (Adult any age) All venues (55 seconds)
    (Annoyed by another dog, Bette tries to give him the brush off)

VANESSA (1) 67
    (Dramatic) (From FORGETTING TO FORGIVE by Glenn Alterman)
    All venues (50's to 70's) (1 minute 12 seconds)
    (Vanessa, saddened by getting older, tells her son what her life was like when she was young and attractive)

RENE 68
    (Dramatic) (Teenager)
    All venues 1 minute 15 seconds)
    (At a party one of Rene's friend offers her some drugs)

CECI 69
    (Dramatic) (20's) All venues (1 minute)
    (Ceci tells off her drunk boyfriend after he kills an animal while driving her car)

SHARON 70
    (From DITMAS by Glenn Alterman)
    (Serio-comedic) (40's to 50's) All venues (55 seconds)
    (A slightly drunk woman talking to the man who helped her after she fell down)

VANESSA (2) 71
    (From FORGETTING TO FORGIVE by Glenn Alterman)
    (Dramatic) All venues (50's to 70's) (50 seconds)
    (Vanessa tells her son why she tried to commit suicide.

JEN 72
    (Dramatic) (30's to 40's) All venues (1 minute)
    (Jen is in an unhappy relationship and here she discusses her ideas about the way out)

WENDY 73
    (Dramatic) (30's to 50's) Agent's office, auditions with longer audition time (2 minutes 16 seconds)
    (After seeing a woman who might be dead Wendy decides to do something rather drastic)

SHE (2) 74
    (From THE KINDNESS OF ENEMIES by Glenn Alterman) (Serio-comedic) (Adult any age) All venues (1 minute 23 seconds)
    (After meeting a man at a bar and going home with him, SHE tells him why she won't give him her phone number)

KAREN 75
    (Serio-comedic) (40's to 60's) All venues (55 seconds)
    (Karen anxiously tries to get her husband to help her with something important)

LITTLE LISA 76
    (Dramatic) (10 to teenager) All venues (1 minute 45 seconds)
    (Little Lisa has a dream where she sees her mother in heaven)

CEIL 77
    (Dramatic) (50's to 70's) (1 minute 7 seconds)
    (Ceil talks about visiting her grandson and her husband)

CHAPTER 6

MEN'S MONOLOGUES

JAKE 81
    (From INSIDE by Glenn Alterman)
    (Dramatic) (50's to 60's) Agent's office, auditions with longer audition time (2 minutes 12 seconds)
    (Jake tells an actor he's met on a movie set how the Aids crisis affected him)

JACOB 83
    (Serio-comedic) (Adult- any age)
    All venues (1 minute 21 seconds)
    (Jacob shares a terrifying experience he had just a few days after he was born)

STEVE 84
    (Comedy) (Mid-20's to early 40's)
    All venues (1 minute 50 seconds)
    (Steve tries to pick up a woman at Happy Hour at a bar with unexpected results)

JOHN 85
    (From TRESPASSED by Glenn Alterman)
    (Dramatic) (30's to 40's)
    All venues (1 minute 17 seconds)
    (John tells his friend Tom how his sister protected him from their physically abusive parents)

BARRY 86
    (From NOBODY'S FLOOD by Glenn Alterman)
    (Dramatic) (30's to 40's)
    All venues (1 minute 30 seconds)
    (Barry tells his parents about the last time he saw his brother)

HERMAN 87
    (Dramatic) (25 to 45) Agent's office, for longer audition times (2 minutes 27 seconds)
    (After leaving a store, Herman sees a man lying on the ground in serious condition)

LOUIS 89
    (Comedic) 30's to 50's) All venues (1 minute 15 seconds)
    (Louis has an erotic moment with a woman sitting at a table.)

CARL 90
    (Serio-comedic) (Teenager) All venues (1 minute)
    (Carl asks his younger brother to return the money he stole from their mother)

HE 91
    (From BENCHMARKS by Glenn Alterman)
    (Dramatic) (30's to 60's)
    All venues (1 minute 17 seconds)

TED 92
  (HE has just met TELLY at a bus stop. Here he tries
  to convince her why she should take the next bus)

  (From TIME WOUNDS ALL HEELS by Glenn
  Alterman)
  (Dramatic) (50's to 70's)
  All venues (55 seconds)
  (Ted advises his young business partner why he needs
  to settle down in life)

NICKY 96
  (Comedy) (Adult- any age) (Any age)
  All venues (1 minute)
  (Nicky explains why he is so obsessed with his own
  beautiful voice)

CHARLIE 94
  (Dramatic) (30 to 40)
  All venues (1 minute)
  (Charlie tells his wife what it's like seeing her again
  after being in prison for five years)

RONALD 95
  (Dramatic) (30's to 40's)
  All venues (1 minute 30 seconds)
  (After another sleepless night, Charlie talks about
  what haunts him)

MARK 96
  (Comedy) (30 to 50)
  All venues (1 minute 25 seconds)
  (After bringing a co-worker home to have sex for the
  first time, Mark tells her what a terrific time he's had)

MEL 97
  (From DITMAS by Glenn Alterman)
  (Dramatic) (30's to 50's)
  All venues (1 minute 20 seconds)
  (Mel tells a former schoolmate how his life has
  changed- dramatically)

HERB 98
  (From IN THE BAG by Glenn Alterman)
  (Comedic) 40's to 50's
  All venues (1 minute 42 seconds)
  (Herb tells his friend how one of his patients came
  on to him- in full drag)

SEBASTIAN 100
    (From THE LAST KEY by Glenn Alterman)
    (Dramatic) (30's)
    All venues (1 minute 22 seconds)
    (Sebastian tells a new arrival how he ended up in Key West)

TED (2) 101
    (From TIME WOUNDS ALL HEELS by Glenn Alterman)
    (Dramatic) (50's to 70's)
    All venues (1 minute)
    (Ted tells his partner what he's discovered on some security cameras he just installed in his home)

SON 102
    (From FORGETTING TO FORGIVE by Glenn Alterman)
    (Dramatic) (late 40's to lat 50's)
    All venues (1 minute 23 seconds)
    (Son realizes that he and his mother have similar experiences with the men in their lives)

MR. ANONYMOUS 103
    (Dramatic) (Adult- any age)
    All venues (1 minute 20 seconds)
    (A man talks about his life of anonymity)

RANDY 104
    (From THE VIEW by Glenn Alterman)
    (Serio-comedic) (20's to 30's)
    All venues (55 seconds)
    (Randy tells a mountain ranger about the last time he saw his brother-in-law)

STAN 105
    (Dramatic) (30's to 50's)
    All venues (1 minute 6 seconds)
    (After being caught with an under age girl, Stan tries to explain to his wife how it happened)

ROB 106
    (Dramatic) 30'a to 40's)
    All venues (1 minute 4 seconds)
    (After his son has committed a horrific crime, Rob tries to apologize)

GENE 107
    (Serio-comedic) (Mid 40's to 60)
    All venues
    (1 minute 30 seconds)
    (Gene, a drag queen, talks to a shy male escort)

SKIPPER 108
    (From THE LAST KEY by Glenn Alterman)
    (Dramatic) (Mid 20's to 30's)
    All venues (55 seconds)
    (Skipper tells a new friend how he ended up in Key West)

JOHN 109
    (From INSIDE by Glenn Alterman)
    (Dramatic) (Mid 30's to mid 50's)
    Agent's office, auditions with longer audition time
    (2 minutes 45 seconds) (John tells a man he just met where he's been for the last fourteen years)

SEARS 111
    (From TRESPASSED by Glenn Alterman)
    (Serio-comedic) (30's to 40's)
    All venues (1 minute 24 seconds)
    (Sears, a bad cop, prepares his married girlfriend for a police investigation)

ZACK 112
    (From THE HIGH LOW LIFE by Glenn Alterman)
    (Serio-comedic)
    (25 to 30)
    All venues (1 minute 40 seconds)
    (Zack, a druggie, tells his girlfriend how he's going to be famous)

Overdone Monologues 115
Permissions 117
About the Author 119

Introduction

When I received an invitation from my publishers, Smith and Kraus, to write another book I was delighted. I'd written twenty-nine books already and felt that was enough, but when I received their invitation, I thought "Yes, one more, thirty!" I hadn't written a book of monologues in a number of years and felt this was the perfect time. I have so many stories I'd like to tell and so many characters I'd like to explore. At this point of my writing career, I believe I know what actors are looking for at their auditions. I've given monologue coaching seminars all around the world and spoken with many actors on the subject. I've had countless discussions with actors about what they are specifically are looking for in a monologue for an audition, and what they're looking for in a monologue book. I've been in touch with many casting directors and agents over the years and have asked them what they specifically look for at monologue auditions. Many of their comments are included in this book.

With the completion of this book I've written *over one thousand original monologues*. That also includes monologues that were cut from my published and produced plays. In those cases I occasionally make small adjustments to the monologues to make them monologue-audition ready.

As a playwright (Glennaltermanplaywright.com) I'm a member of many playwriting/actors groups. Every monologue in this book has had a "trial run" in one of these groups. I've listened carefully to the feedback they received, especially from actors.

Monologue auditions, as many of you are aware, seem to

17

be requiring shorter and shorter monologues for auditions these days. I know that many actors find this annoying and frustrating. I feel your pain. Writing shorter monologues and finding short monologues from my plays that will be effective for auditions can be tough. A previous book that I wrote for Smith and Kraus "101 One-Minute Monologues", was one of the most difficult books I'd ever written. As an actor, I'm sure you know finding a one-minute monologue that has a beginning, middle and end, an emotional arc, and an interesting story is extremely hard to find. Try writing them, it's a real challenge. I believe for the most part I've succeeded in that task.

I wanted this, my thirtieth book, to be an instructional book on everything you'll need to know to find, prepare, and perform your selected monologues for auditions as well as a strong book of monologues for all auditions. The bottom line is you want to find material that "sells you and that can perform to the best of your ability," so you can book that play or film, get that agent, and impress that casting director and theater company.

As you'll also discover, I've reached out to some of the top theater, T.V. and film casting directors and agents to give their opinions on what it takes to give a winning monologue audition. Some of their responses were familiar to me, but I have to admit I was surprised at several of them. You learn something every day.

I'm hoping you'll find this book of value to you with your auditions. In response to your e-mails and comments at seminars I have included many one-minute monologues and monologues from produced and published plays for your auditions in this book. I hope you find what you're looking for here.

Good luck with those auditions!

Glenn Alterman

Chapter 1

All About Monologues

What Is a Monologue?

The word monologue comes from the Greek, meaning "alone, solitary." Webster defines the word monologue as "a dramatic soliloquy," "a long speech." It is a speech presented by a single character to express their thoughts out loud.

There are many types of monologues. Some are spoken directly to the audience. Others try to create the impression that the actor is alone, talking to himself. Some monologues occur when the character is talking to another person or group of people. There is another group of monologues where the character is talking to an imaginary person. The character may be saying things that he's/she's always wanted to say or didn't have the courage to say, or perhaps is preparing to say at a future time. I tried to include ALL these types of monologues in this book.

Why Actors Need Monologues

The reason that casting directors, agents, and theater companies request a monologue audition is to give them some idea of your talent, and, for casting purposes, your type.

The audition monologue is an important marketing tool that can get you a job, an agent, or a role in a play or movie. Every actor should have a wide range of well-rehearsed monologues ready. The last thing you want is to have to prepare a monologue at the last minute for an audition. New monologues should be added to your repertoire on a *regular basis*. Monologues get stale quickly from over use. I'm often amazed how my musical theater students have over one hundred songs ready for their auditions, but only a handful of monologues prepared.

At it's best, the monologue audition is an appetizer of your talent. It's a one or two minute presentation of your taste and skill. You want to find material that excites you, that you enjoy performing. You want to go to each monologue audition with enthusiasm both about yourself as an actor, and about the material that you've selected to perform for the audition. That enthusiasm is contagious.

Selecting a monologue is a pro-active challenge. It's one of the few times that you select what it is you want to perform; you are in charge. You're not waiting for anyone to "give" you anything. You have control of what you want to perform and how you want to perform it.

Types Of Monologue Auditions

For A Specific Play

The preliminary audition for many plays is the monologue audition. Before you get to read from the actual play, they require actors to come to a first audition prepared with anything from a one-minute monologue to two short monologues. They expect you to select monologues that are appropriate for the play you're auditioning for. If that goes well, and you are right for one of the roles, you'll receive a call back where you get to read directly from the play.

The Agent's Office Monologue Audition

You have been notified by the talent agent's office that the agent would like to meet with you for "a general." This is just a meet and greet for them to get to know you and for you to get to know the agent.

Usually they'll ask you to prepare a one or two monologues

for the interview. Hopefully, you have a couple of well-rehearsed and not stale monologues ready to go. If not, you may have to really move on this. If the interview is a week or so away, you have sufficient time to get it together. If it's tomorrow, you're in trouble. In that situation it's best to see if you can re-schedule the appointment for a later time when you feel you'll be ready. An agent appointment is too valuable an opportunity to squander by just throwing something together over night. You don't want your audition to be about trying to remember what the next line in the monologue is.

When you go to the office try to be professional and friendly. Aside from performing the monologues you'll be meeting the agents in the office. They'll be interviewing you to see if you'll be a good fit for their particular office.

For Auditions At Networking Facilities

There are several companies called networking facilities that now offer agent/actor introductions and auditions for a small fee. You are not guaranteed anything from this arrangement other than the opportunity to meet with the agent or casting director. In New York companies like Actors Connection, One on One, Green Room, offer these services. They can be a helpful way to make industry contacts. They usually ask you to bring in a "short monologue." A short monologue can be anywhere from 2 minutes to 3 minutes.

The Casting Director Interview

Some casting directors have "general interviews" where they meet new talent. This is less common then the agent interviews. Generally casting directors meet new actors at auditions that they've held for particular projects. The casting director will occasionally be willing to see an actor that an agent has recommended, or, in some cases, from a photo that an actor had e-mailed to the casting director. These days mailing photos to agents doesn't get the response it use to. At one time actors mailed their picture and resumes and waited to hear back. Many offices don't respond to mailings the way they use too. Find out which ones do. Mailings can be costly.

At these interviews the actor is usually asked to prepare one or two brief monologues. These interviews are generally held in the casting director's office, but can be held at a theater that the casting director is connected to.

The Theater Company General Auditions

Once or twice a year many theater companies hold general auditions to cast roles for their upcoming year. Actors Equity requests that New York Actors Equity resident companies hold these auditions to meet union members for future casting consideration. In some cases the theater company already has a resident company, but might still be looking for a particular type for a role in an upcoming play. In other cases, there is no resident company, so all casting is done through agent submissions, casting director suggestions, and E.P.A.'s (Equity Principal Auditions).

In some cases, sides (from planned upcoming plays) are used at the auditions, but sometimes the actor is asked to prepare either a brief monologue or two contrasting monologues. Monologues that are similar in mood or theme to upcoming plays are recommended for the audition.

Monologue Auditions For Film

Nowadays it seems that more and more film companies, (particularly the independents), are requesting actors bring in a short monologue for their first audition. Rather than giving the actor sides to read from (from their planned film) they ask the actor to choose material that he feels shows off his capabilities. When selecting material for these types of auditions, choose something that doesn't require much movement. Also, the material shouldn't be too emotionally explosive (unless that's called for in the film). When performing the monologue, if you're supposed to be speaking directly to another character, be sure to use the camera as that character.

Monologues For Classroom Work

In acting class a teacher may occasionally suggest a particular monologue for an actor to work on to develop particular skills. For instance he may assign a monologue that demands certain emotions that he feels the actor has trouble expressing. Monologues are also used in class to "stretch" acting muscles. Actors may also bring in their own monologues to explore different acting styles, to stretch or to investigate the works of playwrights that they might not have a shot at in the commercial world.

Chapter 2

Marketing Yourself with the "Right" Monologue

What follows are some suggestions to consider when selecting a monologue.

1. Choose a monologue that is age appropriate. Take into consideration your actual age, but more importantly the age you play (usually get cast).
2. Try to pick a monologue that's active, where the action is happening right now. Select a monologue where your character wants something from the other (unseen) character, where there's a strong need. That being said, don't totally avoid "memory monologues." There are some memory monologues where the images are strong and the writing is emotional. I've seen (and written) some strong memory monologues, some of them are included in this book. They can be very effective. But again, you must discover the need. Why is this character saying this now, and what does he want from the other character he/she's speaking too? In both cases you must figure out what your character wants the unseen character to do, or understand or feel.
3. Find material that showcases your talent, where you're at now in your acting ability. This is not the time to stretch but to showcase what you do best.
4. Unless specifically called for, never do a monologue in a dialect. They want to see and hear who you are now as an

actor. Unless you're Meryl Streep, you can flub the correct pronunciation of some of the words, and that will take the auditor's attention off your performance and start listening to how well you do the dialect. Although some of the monologues in the book may "suggest" a slight dialect (New York-ese, Southern, etc), they are not required to be performed.

5. Find monologues with an emotional arc. Many actors choose material that is just one long angry tirade. That can get boring fast. Material that has you standing up there crying for two minutes doesn't show much, other than you can cry. You want material with transitions, where things change in the different beats. I've tried to include monologues in this books that have arcs, reversals and many different colors. Obviously with a one-minute monologue there isn't going to be a lots of shifts.

6. You don't want to pick monologues that will offend the auditors. Quite often the casting people don't know you and performing with offensive material is the first impression they get of you. The material you choose tells them something about your aesthetic, your taste.

7. Be careful with experimental (non linear, poetic) monologues. Unless they specifically asked for it for their play, you should stick to naturalistic material. They may get confused if the material is too cryptic, which will also take them out of your audition. I realize that sometimes you're auditioning for a play that isn't naturalistic and an experimental/poetic monologue is a better choice. For those particular auditions I've written several poetic/expressionistic monologues that are included in this book.

8. Picking a monologue from a play you've performed in can be tricky. What can be a very exciting moment in the play, may not work as a stand-alone audition piece. You have to remember, in the play there might have been a big buildup to this monologue. It may resonate very differently to the audience in the theater seeing the play, than the casting director

watching your audition. If you decide to do a monologue from a play you've been in for an audition, your preparation should take into account that it's now being performed for an audition. You may have to adjust certain moments.

9. Don't write a monologue for your own audition. I know there are others who will argue with me on this point. But I've discovered that in many cases, what may resonate deeply on a personal level, may not be the best material to showcase your talent. You may be feeling it deeply, but it might not becoming across. When I first started writing monologues, I use to bring in some of my own original material. Back then you had to bring in material from a published play. That is mostly no longer the case today, but there are exceptions. I'm not proud to admit it, but at those auditions I made up a title of a play (and playwright). Never a good thing to do at an audition, --it just adds unnecessary tension. Today, the "plays only" request for auditions have been relaxed and some actors bring in original monologues they've found in original monologue books or material they've written. Some casting directors don't mind you bringing in material you've written, others will ask you if you have something from a produced play. In this book there are both original monologues written specifically for auditions and monologues from my produced and published plays.

10. Don't do monologues that are overdone. Actors often bring in the same monologue classics that the casting director have seen a million times. Yes, they are great monologues, but you can be more effective at your audition if you perform something they haven't seen. Tell them a story they haven't heard. Hopefully you can entertain them as well as showcase your talent. There is a list of many overdone monologues at the end of this book.

11. When you are picking material, pick something that makes you feel something. If it is not special to you, it won't be special for them. Your enthusiasm, excitement about the

material you're presenting is contagious. If it's not exciting for you, it most likely will not be for them.

12. Don't audition with a monologue for too long, they get stale quickly. When you find yourself going on automatic pilot, find new ones.

Chapter 3

Rehearsing Your Monologues For Auditions

1. If the monologue is from a play, read the play, see where the monologue fits into the story.
2. Once you have selected a monologue, read it through from beginning to end. It's usually best to be seated and relaxed. Take your time. Don't push, or rush, just read it. Don't try to "act it," just say the words in an unaffected manner. See what "pops" for you; what feelings, impulses you're feeling. This initial read through is invaluable, stay open to what you're feeling.
3. After giving some thought to what you just read, read it through again. This time if you feel an impulse to say a line or a word a certain way, do it. Try not to judge what you're doing, just play.
4. For the next run through of the piece if you feel an urge to stand up, then do. If not, remain seated. As you're reading it through, allow your body to respond. Again, there is no obligation to "do" anything. If you wish to stand at a certain moment, then do so. If you feel an impulse to say a line with a certain emotion, go ahead. Don't try to act a line or even a word the way you did it in the previous read-through. If it feels right to repeat, allow it, but don't force it. You want to remain as *spontaneous* as you can.
5. Next, think about your character. Where is he/she coming from before they started to speak? If the piece is from a play, let the story in the play guide you. If it's an original

monologue, allow your imagination to create a scenario.

6. Write down any adjectives that describe your character at the very beginning of the monologue.

7. At some point you'll need to decide who your character is speaking to. If the monologue is from a play, you'll need to note who the other character is in the play. What is their relationship to your character?

8. Whether it's from a play or an original piece, you'll need to "personalize the other person." For example, if, in the play, the script tells you, you're talking to the "the Captain," imagine who the captain might be in your "real life." Who do they remind you of, who comes to mind? Your father? Your third grade teacher? A priest you've talked to for guidance? Imagine them standing in front of you, picture them there. If the person from your real life doesn't feel right, then try someone else. As you rehearse, if someone else from your life comes to mind, picture them, see what happens.

9. Start thinking about "why are you speaking?" What is the goal of your character, the objective? What is it you're trying to get from that other person? You may notice that at some point in the monologue there is a shift. The character may realize something and pivot, change their mind. We do that all the time in life, so can the characters we portray.

10. You should start noticing if there are any emotional shifts or beats during the monologue. It's helpful to note where they occur on your script. Characters, like people, can have a shift in mood when something occurs to them while speaking. I always encourage actors to look for these beats in a monologue because it tells us something about the character

11. It's good to notice where your character is at the end of the monologue. Once again, write down any adjectives that describes if there has been a change.

12. Always look for the emotional arc of your character in the monologue. See where the character starts out emotionally and notice how their mood changes, depending on what

their saying (or in some cases, not saying).

13. As you continue rehearsing the monologue, you'll start to notice that you've memorized much of the material just by repeating it. This is the best way to memorize.

14. At a certain point, after you've been rehearsing a while, you should set aside one rehearsal to make sure you have all the word memorized.

15. Spontaneity. Spontaneity. Spontaneity. After you've rehearsed, are fully memorized, and feel you've done all the work you've needed, you should let it go- and trust that the work you've done in rehearsal will pay off at the audition. The auditors don't want to see a speech, they want to see something that looks like it's being said for the *first time*. If you've been methodical in the way you've worked on the monologue, it will live inside you and when you're ready to perform it, it will be there.

16. Preparation. Preparation. Preparation. After you've done all your work at home on the monologue and are ready to audition there are some basic things to keep in mind on audition day.

    a. Always show up at least twenty minutes before your audition time.

    b. Even if you see someone you know at the audition, this not a time to socialize. Just say hello and that's it.

    c. You want to find a place where you can let go of your day and just focus on the monologue. I realize that at some auditions you might be seated with a room filled with other actors. Perhaps you can find a hallway where you can be alone with your thoughts, or even a bathroom will work.

    d. When you've found a private area, you want to breathe, relax and allow your mind to enter the world of the piece you're going to perform.

e. Think about your character, what he/she wants. *Softly* say the words of the monologue to yourself. Don't push, don't act it fully. Just allow yourself to enter the world of the character and who he/she is talking too (the person you've personalized in rehearsal.) When you're satisfied, do a speed through of the lines- softly, a couple of times.

f. The last thing you want to do in your preparation is picture yourself going into the audition room confident and relaxed.

g. Take a few more deep breaths and go back to the waiting area and wait for your name to be called. Again, don't socialize! Stay focused, in the zone, until you walk in the audition room.

h. When called, enter the audition room, smile, and by the way you carry yourself, let them know that you're the right actor for the job.

i. After you've told them what the monologue is from, take a moment for yourself- and just begin.

j. If there are 2 monologues, announce what both of them are from at the beginning.

k. After you've finished the monologue(s), take a moment, smile and say thank you.

l. If they wish to talk to you after, just remain positive, open and confident.

m. After the interview is over, say thank you, and exit as confidently as when you entered.

n. When the audition is over, it's over. I realize that at times it may be difficult, but LET IT GO and continue on with your day. Don't over-analyze everything that went on in the audition room. Get ready for the next one. And there always is a next one!

Chapter 4

Casting Director's Insights on Monologue Auditions

What follows are some insights casting directors that I interviewed had to offer on monologue auditions (and in some cases, all auditions). I appreciate their taking the time to share their advice. You may notice that some of them offer similar advice, those are things you should pay particular attention too.

James Calleri

I see auditions/monologues as getting to know the actors- equate it to a first date. No one gets cast just from doing a monologue, you do get to go to the next step though an audition or meeting for a specific project.

Make sure the other person in the piece although they are not present in the room is clear and vivid for you. It is all about responding to the reactions from the other person. This is what propels you to keep speaking. Those reactions and responses from the imaginary partner must be strong and specific.

Alan Filderman

I notice the actor's speech skills, that they maintain a comfortable body language, and an emotional connection to the text.

Diane Heery

I look for an actor who makes me forget that I'm watching an audition! The actor should be fully involved in his character without projecting that he/she is conscious of being watched. Actors should remember that just the ***choice*** of monologue tells a lot about how you perceive yourself and how you present your talent to others. No one forced you to use that particular piece; it should be something that "speaks" to you.

Arnold Mungioli

An actor who has done his or her homework and made choices that are bold yet logical.

An actor who is confident -- not afraid of doing a monologue or annoyed by the request.

An actor who has made an ACTIVE choice and is using the words he or she is speaking to *play an action* -- not just narrating a story or "telling" us something.

An actor who does monologues as part of his trade and enjoys that work -- not an actor who had to go out and pick a monologue to do and memorize it and work it up in the time since he or she got the appointment.

Sandra Steiner

I look for actors who have done their homework on the monologue. They should be totally believable for that entire 2 minutes.

I can always tell when an actor has done the same monologue for too long. It no longer feels spontaneous.

Actors should have many monologues prepared that they use for auditions. I usually suggest having 5 or 6 monologues of different varieties.

It's probably best to work with an acting coach or a teacher on your monologues. I can only imagine that working on them by yourself might be difficult.

Breanna Benjamin

Is the actor the character? Has he checked out of the physical surroundings and into the world of the character?"

Adrienne Stern

Speech patterns, character development, ease and flow with diction, complete awareness of their surroundings, comfortable body language.

CASTING DIRECTORS—ON THE MOST COMMON MONOLOGUE MISTAKES

James Calleri

I feel one of the biggest mistakes actors make during the monologue audition is addressing the auditioner during the monologue. It makes me feel like I need to be there for the actors, and yet I'm trying to evaluate their work.

I find that most pieces are too long. When they are I get bored and want to move on.

Alan Filderman

Feeling nervous and not prepared is a problem for many actors. Many actors do monologues that are not "right" for them (i.e. a woman in her early 20's doing Blanche).

Doing a monologue that is so "out there" that the auditor spends all of his time and energy trying to figure out what the hell the monologue is about.

Doing a monologue without having read THE ENTIRE PLAY that the monologue is from is a mistake actors often make.

Taking a scene and removing the other character and calling it a monologue", doesn't work.

Arnold Mungioli

The most common mistake is actors failing to make an active choice with their monologues. Most commonly they choose some version of "to tell", i.e.: "to let the person I am speaking to know this or that..." or "to explain to the person I am speaking to..." -- it is invariably a weak choice and gives them no support in the audition. "

It is always best to present yourself with material from roles in which you could realistically be cast! Be imaginative in your choice of material, but do not be ridiculous and out-of-touch!

Adrienne Stern

Telling you what their monologue is about or who wrote it.
Forgetting their lines halfway thru and not knowing how to fake it.
Choosing to do an accent when one has not been asked for.

Breanna Benjamin

Preparing in front of the auditioners. We don't want to see you "take a moment" and exercise or deep breathe, or meditate. Just do your audition material.

Diane Heery

The piece should have at least 3 transitions in it and be "*age-appropriate.*"

Robert Longston

Make sure when you enter the audition room that you bring a positive energy. You may be nervous- but don't show it!

If you're doing 2 monologues for us, always tell us the names of the plays they're from (or if they're original monologues).

It's best to name the two monologues first, rather than saying the name of monologue one and after, telling us what the second monologue is from.

Also, just take a quick moment between the two monologues and move on to the second one. Don't take too long.

Interview With Casting Director Risa Bramon Garcia On Monologue Auditions

1. *What do you feel are the most important things actors need to know when selecting and preparing monologues for auditions?*

It's imperative to find a piece of material that resonates with you. Something that touches you emotionally, that stirs you, that you can relate to. It can be anything from Sam Shepard to Shakespeare. And it takes time to dig for pieces and to try them on. This may seem like a simple process, but it's one that demands some care, thought, and consideration.

Actors tend to want things to happen quickly and immediately. And like everything else with this work you do, finding the right material requires some work. Work that can be fun and exciting, as well as challenging.

In terms of preparation, you have to get inside it and you have to find where it lives in you. You have to make it personal, understand exactly what you're saying and what you want out of it. I find that actors often tend to want to talk a monologue at someone, rather than make it something deeply and personally urgent (whether it be light or heavier), that need to affect another person. Words that absolutely have to be said right here, right now. And words that must be spoken to someone. You're not talking to the wall, the air, the ground, or the trees outside the window. You're not lost in memory, in reverie, or thought. You are not alone in your experience. You want something from someone, whether that person is there or not, and you use this text to make that happen. Think of it as this: you want something so badly that you can't stop talking, which is why you have this organization of words that are imperative. There's no space for anyone else to say anything until you declare or reveal something, until you tell your story, until you get out everything you have to say.

And then you have to have a really clear want, need, objective- whatever you want to call it- and pursue that actively. You're not just telling the story, you're making something happen.

When you find a monologue that stirs your heart and your imagination, and when you get really specific about what you're saying and why, when you know who you're talking to and talking about, and you drive that forward until you get what you want, you'll drop into it and it will just flow out of you. It will feel like life, not a "monologue."

A monologue is like a jazz riff. It's a piece of music, isolated, for the moment, from the rest of the orchestra. Something that has a life of its own.

2. *What specifically do you look for when an actor does a monologue for you?*

I want to reframe this question because I don't ever want an actor to "do a monologue for me." I want the actor to be significantly involved in his/her experience, to be compelled to keep talking, to have a strong point of view, and to get what he/she wants. When the focus is on that, not in performing a monologue or getting my attention by knowing all the words, when the focus is on actively engaging with another human being and driving a big "want" forward, the actor will be using a series of crafted words to actively engage in the pursuit of something.

That's what I want. I want to be part of that experience. I want to be invested in that person and I want them to get what they desperately want. I want to lose myself in their story.

We often work with monologues in class and the first thing actors tend to do is to make their monologues about themselves. They get lost in reverie, in their heads, and in memory and thought. Well that's not life. When we talk and talk, it's because we are deeply and urgently compelled to say something, even if it's a speech. There's a huge intent there. When we shift the intent on to someone, outward, it changes. When we play with the circumstances in order to learn something new, it changes. It frees us. When we allow ourselves to drop into the moment, this "chunk of words" becomes a compelling and active experience. For everyone. It's crazy how that works.

I also want to encourage actors to write their own pieces.

We are big believers at our Studio in actors creating work, and we have actors write monologues all the time. It's a powerful exercise out of which often comes fantastic material. We recently worked on a monologue project in one of my classes, culminating in shooting 21 pieces. In the end, these didn't feel like my lungs; they were human experiences.

3. *What are the biggest mistakes actors make at monologue auditions?*

As I said, actors tend to act alone. Actors tend to forget that they're speaking words, words that are a tool, an instrument with which to express their emotional life and their deep need, a way with which to connect to another human being or a group of people. When the focus is on that, the monologue turns into a vessel for communication, connection, and action.

And, as with everything else you do in preparing material, you have to remember that it's about getting ready for that moment of presence. It's about allowing all of the preparation to turn into the urgency and discovery in the moment. So you're not reciting a chunk of words. You're putting thoughts together (quickly or slowly or anything in between) to say something imperative. Right then. Right there. As you allow yourself to be free enough to know your words- which comes from being clear in your objective, specific in the world you've created, and grounded in a strong emotional place, you will be in the rush of discovery. This monologue will grab hold of you, and then it will grab hold of us.

RISA BRAMON GARCIA
Advice For Monologue and All Auditions; a Check List

Here is a list of important things to always keep in mind for your monologue (and ALL) auditions.

1. Come to do the work you love so much, not to please or get our approval.
2. Enter with certainty. Don't give up your power as soon as the door opens.
3. Play on a level playing field. We're all figuring it out. Together.
4. Make no excuses whatsoever. Leave your baggage outside. Better yet, leave it at home.
5. Make the room your own. It will make us so much more comfortable and engaged.
6. Ask questions only when you truly need answers. "Do you have any questions?" is usually another way of saying, "Are you ready?" You aren't required to have one.
7. Make decisions and take responsibility for the ones you make.
8. Don't apologize. Ever. For anything.
9. Know that your homework is done. Now let your preparation meet the moments.
10. Don't mime or busy yourself with props, activity, or blocking. Keep it simple; the only thing that matters is you in the moment..
11. Require no stroking, coddling, or love. We're there to work. Don't take it personally when we're not touchy-feely. Know that we love actors and that's truly why we're here.
12. What you bring in reflects how you're received, so bring joy, conviction, and ease, and our hearts will open.
13. Share your artistry above all else.

Remember that we're all human in those rooms, and you can affect us on an emotional level. It's what we all really want. That's your job. You being fully present, truthful, personal, and vulnerable is going to give us the ammunition we need to champion you with all our hearts. We all desperately want you to do great work. We're rooting for that every time you walk into the room. You show up and do your fullest, deepest work, and we'll slay dragons for you and follow you anywhere.

RISA BRAMON GARCIA is a director, casting director, teacher, and partner in The BGB Studio, a space for revolutionary acting training and a creative home for Artists. http://bramongarcia-braun.com/

Chapter 5

Monologue Guidelines For This Book

To let you know which monologues are best suited for you there are guidelines at the top of each page to assist you.

1. Many of the monologues in this book are from PLAYS THAT RECEIVED PRODUCTIONS AND PUBLICATIONS. That information will appear first in parenthesis and state the name of the play in caps.

    Example- (From NAME OF PLAY)

2. Next will be the type of EMOTIONAL LIFE IN THE MONOLOGUE.

    Example- (Dramatic) (Serio-comedic) or (Comedic)

3. Next are SUGGESTED AGE RANGE for the monologue. If it's from a play, I list what the age of the character was. Otherwise I suggest an age range that might be believable for that character.

    If you like a monologue and there is no reference in the material as to the characters age, you can select it. These are just SUGGESTED age ranges.
    Example (20 to 30) (Teenager) (Adult)

4. Next is the RUNNING TIME of the monologues. We've timed each piece down to the very second. This can be important in the 1 and 2 minute monologue auditions, especially when there is someone at the audition with a stop watch. Each actor performs a piece at their own pace, so

there is some flexibility here. You may want to time yourself if you feel you may be timed at the audition.

5. I've indicated the VENUE for each monologue so you know where the piece can be performed. ALL VENUES (most of the monologues in this book) means that the piece can be performed for all theater auditions, Agent's office auditions, as well as TV and film auditions.

The LONGER (over 2 minutes) monologues are generally best for the Agent's office auditions, where they ask for a "short monologue" with no time restraint. The longer monologues are also good for classroom work, where you're allotted more time. None of the monologues in this book are over 3 minutes long.

Women's Monologues

MARLA

(Dramatic)
(30's to 50's)
(1 minute 22 seconds) All venues
(After being in a serious car accident with her husband, Marla vents her feelings)

You insisted, INSISTED! But I said, "No, don't!" Why don't you EVER listen to me, huh?! Since day one, our first date, you always... !! Why do I even bother? I could yell forever, and... ! (A bit softer) I don't even know what I'm saying anymore. (A half smile) This is the longest you've ever let me yell at you, you know that? . ----WELL YELL BACK AT ME, GOD DAMN IT! (A beat, softer) Kids don't know yet. I couldn't tell 'em, the holidays. Said you're out of town, working.

(Sitting down, softer) Look at you, what a mess. ...Okay, fine, I'm scared, happy? (Leaning in, softer) Why couldn't you listen to me, just once? We could have taken a cab. But no, you had to...! God-damn you!

(A beat, softer) The Adlers called, asked how you were doing. If there's anything they...

(Leaning in, sadly) Look, I know you're in there. Know you can hear me. Well you listen -good. Cause I'm never gonna say this again. (Softer) You... are my life, my everything. I need you, damn it. Now you come back, (smiling) I need someone to fight with! Look, you always loved to win. Well you won, you son of a bitch! Now sit the hell up in that bed and yell at me! SCREAM! (Softly) ... Come back you bastard. (Softer) Fight with me. Yell!

MARY

(Dramatic)
(Late 20's to 40's)
(1 Minute 22 seconds) All venues
(Mary yearns to connect with a guy she sees on the other side of the dance floor. An inner monologue.)

Whatiya lookin' at, huh? Yeah, you over there. You, way over there, other side of the dance floor. You, big guy, with them big blue eyes. You, who's tryin' so hard not to look interested. Like you don't even see me, right. But you do. I can tell; *women know.*

I mean if you were a real gentleman, you wouldn't just sit and stare. You'd come over here, say hello, tell me your name. You'd ask me if I wanted to dance. But you won't. Guys like you never do. You'll just sit there with your pals, talkin', checkin' out the ladies. Wasting time, another Saturday night at the Union Hall. I never understand it. Why? Why are you sitting there and me here. Why can't you just take a chance? We ain't kids anymore, y'know. (Suddenly, furious) WHY, HUH?! WHAT ARE YOU SO DAMN AFRAID OF?! (Calming down, softly) Look... look, I'm as lonely as you are. I know how it feels. And I also know what it feels like to walk home alone, another Saturday night. Wishing it was different. (Looking over at him, more hopeful) But we could talk, have a real good time, get to know each other. We could laugh and dance and... (Then, looking in his direction, surprised) What? ...What are you doin'? You comin' over here; are you?! You're lookin' right at me. You gonna say hello? (Very hopeful) I think.... I-THINK-YOU-ARE. (Joyful) WELL, YEAH, YES! COME-ON-OVER! (Softer) You just keep walkin', Mister. (Smiling, happier) Just keep right on walkin'. – Yeah, YEAH, (Big smile) I'm-right-here!

HELENA

(Serio-comedic)
(30's to 40's)
(1 minute and 13 seconds) All venues
(Helena makes a plan with a young man to meet him at a motel later that night)

(Softly, seductively, a polite smile) Meet me at the motel, okay? You know where it is, over on route nine. And don't tell no one. Not your girlfriend, your boss, no-one. Just go there, rent a room, check in, get undressed, and... sit on the edge of the bed --and wait. Just strip and leave the lights off, understand? No, leave the *bathroom* light on. And the bathroom door wide open, so I can see you there on that bed, waiting for me when I get there. Now will you do that, huh, will ya? 'Cause if you do, if you do exactly what I say, something will happen in that motel room tonight you will never forget. I'll make you happier than any of those wealthy wives that sit around the pool and fawn all over you every damn day. I will make you feel like more of a man than any of those women who eye you here every day in the supermarket when they ask you to cut them some pastrami or Swiss Cheese. ...So just do what I say, okay? Good. We will have ourselves one hell of a good time tonight. (A friendlier smile) Now-- why don't you just shake my hand politely, hand me my order of roast beef, give me a nice, polite, friendly good, bye smile- and go back to work.

TERRY

(From AFTER by Glenn Alterman)
(Comedy)
(Middle aged)
(1 minute) All venues
(Terry makes a confession to a man she's just met at a funeral)

Alright, little confession. This isn't the first time I've gone to a funeral of someone I didn't know. Do it all the time. You see, my husband died last year and we had his service right here, this synagogue. And, I don't know, I just keep coming back. If there's a funeral, like today, I just stop in. Crazy, huh? Generally people don't ask who I am, I just mix in with the crowd. And I get to share some sorrow with them, to commiserate, if you know what I mean. If they do ask who I am, I just tell 'em I knew the deceased from the synagogue. S'just a little white lie.

I really just like going to funerals, I do. Let me tell you, you learn so much, and not only about the deceased. People at funerals are, I don't know, so open, honest, alive. All their feelings right there at their finger tips. I know, s'kinda ironic, huh? People being so alive at a funeral. But they are. And me, I feel alive too when I'm here. Maybe I am just crazy, I don't know. But I don't think so.

CYNDI

(Dramatic)
(30's to early late 40's)
(1 minute 52 seconds) All venues
(Cyndi talks about the night she met Manny in a bar and tried to take him home)

Was four in the morning,
Snyder's just closed.
Me an' Manny was drunk,
        stoned.
Streets were quiet,
        hardly no cars.
So I said,
    "Hey Manny,
        c'mon,
            let's go."
But Manny,
        Manny, said,
            "No."
Then Manny got mean.
Broke a bottle.
I looked,
        saw,
            said, "Manny, put that down."
But Manny,
        he just said, "No."
I said,
    (Sweeter) "C'mon, c'mon, let's go,
            back to my place.
        Have a real good time, real *stoned!*
C'mon, Manny, let's go!"
But Manny,
        he kept just sayin', "No!"
Then it starts to rain.
        Rains real hard,

                                pours.
"Manny, I said,
        "S'go back to my place,
                    where it's nice and warm.
                        I'll take real good care a ya.
But Manny put that broke beer bottle up to my face.
And he had *devils* in his eyes.
An' I knew
                knew--- he was gonna *cut me!*
                        Just like Joe.
                                        Just like Joe.
And so I said "Manny,
        Don't; no!"
Knew he'd cut me,
                then say he's sorry.
Just like Joe.
Just like Joe.
So we just stood there,
        me an' him,
                        four A.M.
                                    gettin' soaked in the rain.
(A beat)
        No man writes my story.
        No guy pays my way.
Had no choice.
Grabbed that bottle,
            (Angrily) An' I CUT Manny's face!
(Softer) Then Manny,
        he cried, cried like a *baby.*
An' I turned,
            just walked away.
Left him in the rain.
Hell, Manny, he don't even know my name.
So I left him
                    bleeding,
                                crying in pain.

(A beat, softer) Was a quiet night.
Hardly any cars out.
An' I walked home,
    alone,
          Walked home,
                  in the pouring rain.

MONICA

(Comedic)
(17 to 27)
(1 minute)
(Monica tells her best friend that she knows that she was making out with her ex-boyfriend)

(A slightly forced smile) Upset? Me? Why should I be? I am so over him! Past tense. Turn the page; he's history. But -I gotta admit, I was somewhat surprised, y'know. 'Mean you and me, we both talk and text all the time. (Not smiling, an edge) Just musta skipped your mind, huh?

When Aisha told me she saw two in the movies, making out, like all hot and heavy- I was like wow, really. I was- *surprised.* 'Mean, you bein' my bff, and all that! All that, yeah. But no worries, girl. Water off a ducks back. S'just a bleep on the screen; know what I mean? I wish you two well, hope it works out. You *deserve* each other; birds of a feather.

Well,-- I gotta go, gotta date. New guy, nice, VERY hot. But hey, if it don't work out. I will text you ASAP. (An edge) And in the future, if I have any more, y'know, *throw-a-ways,* you'll be the first to know. Gotta go!

SHERRY

(Comedic)
(20's to 30's)
(2 minutes, 25 seconds) Agent's office auditions, longer auditions, classroom work.

(Sherry loves to meet men at bars and go back with them for fun and what always turns into a surprise ending)

(Sexy, sultry) He told me he was a bad-bad boy. And I wanted him to know I had sympathy for the devil, and was a sucker for man in a suit. Was cocktail hour, we were both in that bar looking for some *take out*. We were making small talk, but our eyes were *giving it away*. He asked me if I wanted another drink. I smiled, said, (playfully) "I'm already intoxicated." I said that, I did. He smiled. (A smile) Game on!

So then I told him about Mitt and how our marriage was falling apart. And he asked if I needed a shoulder to cry on, and I said "Why waste those big shoulders just for tears?" (Smiling) I swear I said that, I did.

Next thing I knew we were flying down a highway in his white charger with naughty thoughts, dirty dreams. Landed back at his place, on his couch, and I said "Let's have another drink." He said "Sure." So I got our drinks, put them on the table and stood there.

I looked at him, said, "Strip. ...Slowly. ...Now." Off came his tie! I smiled. Then his jacket; I smiled even more. Then came his shirt, which he neatly folded on the chair nearby. But before he took his pants off, I said "C'mere." And like a little doggie he did. I handed him our glasses, said, "A toast to good times with happy endings." And we downed our drinks. Slowly he began to take his pants off. He was doing like a little strip-tease for me. We looked at each other, long, lusty stares. As... his eyes started to glaze. I... just... smiled.

(A beat) Well pretty soon I called Tim, he was waiting down stairs. He'd followed us back from the bar. I said, "I'll be right down, hon."

When I got downstairs he asked, "How'd it go?" I said. "Our bad-bad boy is now enjoying a nice nap on the floor with his pants half off. Should be good till morning, I only put one in his drink."

Then I showed Tim his wallet with all those credit cards and all-that cash. Tim smiled, put his arms around me. I snuggled up to him. I love how he smelled. He always smells so good. Then he started the car and we left, went on an all night buying spree! And the next morning we took off for points unknown, in search of new bad-boys, in Never-Never Land.

CHERYL

(Dramatic)
(20's to 30's)
(1 minutes, 15 seconds) All venues
(Cheryl recalls seeing a moment just like this one, growing up. A gentle, inner monologue)

It felt like a scene from a dream. Dream I'd had many times, growing up in foster homes. Living my life with strangers. It was like a memory, but of something that never actually happened.

(A beat) The storm had just stopped. I was standing by the window looking out at the snow, breastfeeding the baby. It was quiet, still, -just as I remembered.

The door opened and he walked in. I turned and smiled. He smiled back, came over, put his arms around us; me and the baby. Then he kissed her on the cheek, gently. Perfect, just as I remembered.

(Smiling) The baby yawned, her fingers, moved just a little. She smiled, went back to feeding, happy, content.

So we stood there, the both of us and the baby, looking out, watching the last of the snowfall. The three of us, that moment, just as I recalled. Those times when I lived in other peoples homes, shared other peoples lives. Always dreaming, always wishing for just this.

It was like a scene from a dream, but this time, this time... it was real.

GINGER

(Serio-comedic)
(Teenager)
(1 minute, 58 seconds) All venues
(Ginger has a life-threatening incident happen while sitting at a table and looking at a boy she likes.)

Gumball, yeah, I swear! I was sitting right here. Yeah, this table, and Bobby was way over there. And he was like, y'know doing a look over at me. But pretending not too. You know how guys do that. So I was like pretending, "Okay, you dick, I don't notice you either!"

He was with (ugly face) Sally, yeah, Sal-ly. Anyway, me and Vanessa are like trying to decide either movie or mall. And we're talkin' when like all of a sudden my gumball got stuck in my throat. YEAH, AND I COULDN'T BREATHE! And suddenly it hit me, "I'M GONNA DIE!" I fell on the floor, started grabbing my throat, like this. (She does.) Swear I was never so scared! Saw STARS, Donna, STARS!

And I look up, and like an angel, Bobby's standing there, looking down at me, like all concerned and everything. And he like lifted me up off the floor, like Superman! And he started doing that Heimglichy... that Heimlich maneuver thing. Y'know where they push in on your stomach real hard with their hands. Then he did it again and again! I WAS SO SCARED! But then - the gumball went flying out of my mouth. Yeah, like a bullet! ---And I could like breathe again. Realized, I'm NOT gonna die!

And Bobby said, (Softly) "Hey, you okay?" He had this look, like he really cared. And I said, (Softly) "Yeah, think I am-- now. Thank you, Bobby." Then I gave him like a real big hug. And then I saw Sally was standing like right behind him. And she said, "We were so scared, Ginger." I'm glad you're okay." And I think I said thanks to her, and gave her a big hug too. Yeah, I did.

And I sat back in my chair, and looked up at Bobby, and smiled, and he smiled, said, "No problem." I picked up the gumball off the floor, put it on the table. And then I grabbed Vanessa's hand and we both left, went to the mall not the movie.

HELENE

(Comedic)
(Mid twenties to early forties)
(2 minutes 25 seconds) Agent's office, longer auditions, classroom work.
(Helene tells her friend Doris of a terrifying incident that happened on her way to meet her fiancé's family)

Heels or flats, should be a simple decision, right? But I mean I was meeting his mother! Wanted to look perfect. But I couldn't make up my mind, Doris, heels or flats.

Now I know Harold hates me in heels. Always thought it's cause I'm taller than him when I wear them. But I look way better in heels!

So anyway, I'm running really late, have to decide. Everything else, my whole outfit- fabulous. Was wearing that new beige Calvin Klein. Jewelry, simple pearls, delicate chain, perfect. Felt I'd be absolutely "mother approved." So finally I thought, "Screw the heels, I'll go with the flats, make Harold happy!" So I put 'em on, grabbed my bag, ran out the door. Started running, I was running late.

So I get to Ninth Avenue and forty-third, see my bus coming, and notice the lights about to change. So I make like a bolt for the bus. And just as I'm crossing Ninth Avenue, just as I'm mid-way, the light changes!

(A beat) I think it must have been an old exhaust pipe. Or something that had just fallen off some car. It was just laying there in the middle of the street. And I tripped on it, could feel myself falling, going down. Think, damn, I'm gonna die! And from the corner of my eye I could see the cars coming up Ninth Avenue, rushing towards me. (Softly) And in that moment, all I could think was how much I loved Harold. And how tragic it was gonna be. And I wondered what he'd tell his mother about me. And I imagined what my new Calvin Klein suit would look after... after... (A beat, softer) I really don't know how it happened. But I got-my-balance-back, I didn't fall! And I was up and running again! A miracle in the middle of Ninth Avenue!

Anyway, I got to the curb, ---just as the cars came flying by. A couple on the corner applauded me, yeah! Some guy said, "Nice, save!" I was a little embarrassed, but I was alive! (A beat) And the craziest thing, the bus was waiting for me. How often does that happen?! So I got on and the driver smiled! I smiled back, said, "Thank you."

Got a seat, sat and looked down at my feet. Was then I realized, if I'd been wearing those Adolfo high heels... The flats saved my life, Harold was right! So I just sat there Doris, on that bus, the whole ride, looking down at my shoes. Crazy, huh?
(A Beat, smiling, softly) Well, I met his mother. She's really very nice. And it went very well; very well, yeah.

TELLY

(From BENCHMARKS by Glenn Alterman)
(Comedic)
(Adult-any age)
(1 minute, 20 seconds) All venues
(While waiting at a bus stop for a bus, Telly begins a harangue to a stranger she just met, about benches.)

Did you know that benches were originally designed for the common people? The upper class got to sit in chairs. Well constructed, probably very expensive, hand made chairs. Got to rest their upper class asses on elegant, well designed, ... Well I assume they were well designed, but most certainly they were comfortable and cushiony. While the poor people sat on hard wooden benches. Just think of it, the indignity! They now knew their place in the world. They were commoners, delegated to "the bench." And so they sat there, perhaps begrudgingly, or, I don't know, maybe just resigned, thinking, SHIT, I'M SITTING ON A GOD-DAMNED BENCH!

And now here we are, you and me, on one of maybe a million benches. You know they're everywhere; benches. Anywhere you go, they're there. And they're not just for the poor anymore. Every country, every park, every bus stop, streets, malls, even in the middle of no where, for no apparent reason, there they are! These wood and cement or wood and metal fixtures. Furniture. Just waiting to be sat on or slept on. Day and night. cold or warm. They're there; waiting for those who are waiting. The weary traveler or the tired or the poor. Or people like us, waiting for a bus. Waiting. Yeah, I know, I've been told, I talk too much; sorry.

SHE

(From THE KINDNESS OF ENEMIES by Glenn Alterman)
(Comedic)
(Adult- Any age)
(1 minute) All venues

(SHE has met HE at a bar at Happy Hour. They've gone home, had sex, and gotten dressed. Here SHE tells HE what she hopes will happen)

(Desperate, anxious) I could learn to love you; I could. And I'd stay here, make your house my home. And you and me, we could have babies, lots and lots of babies; big family. Y'know, I bet you'd be a good parent. Bet we'd both be good parents. And we could get a couple of dogs, yeah, puppies, any breed, doesn't matter. Whatever you like. See, YOU'D be the decision-maker in our family; I'd let you. And if you're allergic to dogs, doesn't matter. We could get- an otter. Why not? 'Mean hey, I LOVE otters! And NO ONE'S allergic to otters, right? We could get like eight otters; have otters everywhere! We could sleep, drink, and eat with all our little otters. And we can name them. Names like Bim and Bam. Have birthday parties for each and every one of them! And there'd be festivities and happiness in our home! Think of it, such joy! And pretty soon, our little otters will have other otters. It'll be OTTER PARADISE!

WE-CAN-DO-THIS, WE CAN! I mean, why not? (A beat) Not that I'm trying to push this on you. It's just an idea.

JACKI

(From PHONE by Glenn Alterman)
(Serio-comedic)
(20's-30's)
(1 minute, 53 seconds) All venues
(Jacki, an attractive young woman, talks about why she got into a relationship with the man she's with- who happens to always be on his phone).

(Not smiling) He's talking- on the phone. As usual. Always, all the time. Talk, talk, talk. Anywhere we walk, he's always on that damn phone. Always talking, but-not to-me. S'almost as if I weren't here. Maybe I'm not. As if I didn't exist. (An edge) Maybe I don't. S'just him and that damn phone! Every once in a while, him letting me know that he's aware I'm even here. Let me tell you, it can get very lonely sometimes. But I've kind of gotten use to it. S'just the way it is.

Hey, I know what this looks like. Someone like me with someone like him. Minute I met him I knew. Knew exactly what I was getting in to. But I was impressed. Hey he's a big man, important. People look up to him!

There certainly weren't many men like him when I was growing up. Was just momma and me. And momma, she hardly ever talked. Just drank. And sat. And stared at the T.V.

And now I'm with him -and his phone. (A small smile) But membership has it's privileges. There's the perks y'know. I live a very comfortable life.

And now here we are seated in this nice, plush restaurant. Pricey menu, expert service. And-- he's still on the phone. Truth is… (Slow seething anger) I could kill him right now; I could. One long cut, ear-to-ear. Pick up this knife from the table and… he wouldn't even know what happened until the blood started pouring out all over this lovely white table cloth. But I bet THEN he'd drop that phone! THEN he'd stop talking and look ONLY AT ME! And I'd just sit here, watch him bleed. Maybe he'd scream—or (a slight smile) gurgle. But he'd just be looking at me, wouldn't he? I'd be the last thing he ever saw. And he wouldn't be on that phone anymore. Disconnected. And for that short time--he'd be all-mine. Maybe I'll do that. Maybe I will. It's a definite possibility.

BETTE

(Comedy)
(Adult)
(55 seconds) All venues
(Annoyed by another dog, Bette decides to tell him off)

(Very annoyed) You; again?! What I tell you, huh? ---Leave-me-alone! Can't you see, I'm sitting and sunning myself? I don't want company! ...Don't just stand there and stare. Find yourself another place, it's a big park! ... Did you hear me?! What, you think this is some kind of a joke? That you can just sniff around... Look, I may not have a pedigree, but I have something you don't have; self worth. 'Means I'm not just crawling around the park day and night hunting for a piece of tail.
...Why am I even bothering? Your drool's giving you away. You couldn't care less. I'd be just another notch on your dog collar. Look, I'm trying to be nice, but I don't want your wet nose anywhere near....! Hey, enough, I'm warning you, my teeth are sharp, and my claws mean business! Now go wag your bushy tail somewhere else. Find yourself some other bitch to bother!

VANESSA (1)

(From FORGETTING TO FORGIVE by Glenn Alterman)
(Dramatic)
(50's to 70's)
(50 seconds) All venues
(Vanessa, saddened by getting older tells her son what life was like for her when she was young and attractive)

I'm vain. I know, I am. Who else would be sitting here with her son looking at old pictures of herself, right after she tried to commit suicide? That my son — is vain! Even your father, that son of a bitch, always used to say, "Vanessa, you're so damn vain." But I had my looks back then, could get away with almost anything, yeah. Men use to look and turn all the time. Meant a lot to me, felt like money in the bank. And all that attention was—a bargaining chip. Could get what you wanted if you were a woman with looks. And I played it for all it was worth. Now when I look in the mirror, I wonder, who's that old woman there? All those wrinkles. Even the fillers can't fill them anymore. Ya can't fill canyons. I want to go back, back to when I was young and beautiful and in control.

RENE

(Dramatic)
(Teenager)
(1 minute, 15 seconds) All venues
(At a party one of Rene's friends offers her some pills that'll get her super high)

I don't know, you really think they're that good? I mean, some kids say they could kill ya. Isn't that crazy? Mindy swore she knew a kid who went out of her mind, like crazy. But you know Mindy, she's such a liar.

My cousin, Carlene, you know her, goes to Erasmus. She took some one night and said it was like the best thing EVER! Went dancing all night. And then she said they went swimming like really late, in NOVEMBER in the lake at Prospect Park! Said it felt so good. She said it was like she'd never felt water before. And that she could HEAR and SEE people's thoughts. AND. IN. COLOR. I mean how do you see peoples thoughts in color?
(A beat) I don't know if I should. 'Mean Carlene's still alive, didn't kill her. But she did kinda freak out the next day. Yeah, tried jumping off the George Washington bridge. Said, she thought she could fly. Guess she just wanted to be in the water again. They took her away to some place somewhere. She was there like a week.

(A beat) Y'know, y'know, I think I'm gonna pass on the pills but thanks. (Smiling) I really don't need to see other people's thoughts in color, I got too many in my own head. ...So uh, why don't we go back to the party, huh? And- thanks for the offer.

CECI

(Dramatic)
(20's)
(1 minute) All venues
(Ceci's drunken boyfriend accidentally murdered an animal on the way home from a party. Here she angrily tells him off)

No, no it was not, it was NOT an accident! I was right there, next to you! You just had to have it, huh? That-one-last-drink! Even though I told you, "John, you had enough." Kept saying "C'mon, Johnny, let's go." But no, you wouldn't have it. Ignored me, Mr Big Man on campus, trying to impress all your frat brothers!

And in the car, when I yelling, "Slow down!" Again, just ignored me! Well I was there-and I saw- and-I-know!

And the worst part YOU JUST KEPT GOING! It was howling, John! That poor thing might be dead. You're a murderer!
(Looking at him, soft anger)---Do you even care?
(A beat) Fine, well here's what's gonna happen. I'm going back. I'm gonna see what you did, if it's even still alive. And I want you out of here when I get back. Just pack your stuff and leave! I don't care where you go. ---And you'll have to walk, walk John, because I'm taking the god-damned car!

SHARON

(From DITMAS by Glenn Alterman)
(Comedic)
(40's to 50's)
(55 seconds) All venues
(After being rescued from a fall in a bar, Sharon, who's slightly tipsy, starts chatting with her rescuer)

(She's slightly drunk, lighthearted) You are a true gentleman, Mel, you are. As you saw, me and Mr. Floor were getting, well, (smiling) y'know, kina intimate. I mean I saw dust balls down there! (Leaning in, playful) Mel, I could tell you such dirty stories about that filthy floor, but I shall spare you. And you wanna know why? 'Cause you saved me, you did...from my fall from grace. That bar stool over there just tipped over and next thing I knew... fall from grace. (Then, suddenly very cozy)---You ever know anybody named Grace, huh Mel? No? Me neither. And it's really such a nice name, Grace, y'know? I mean I've known some Graziella's, and maybe a few Bethany's and... blah, blah, blah. Listen to me go on. Talkin' like we're old beer buddies. And you really don't know me, I mean not really. I mean takes more than a fall from a chair to ruffle these feathers. Yeah. I am one tough woman. I'm from Brooklyn; Brooklyn tough! (Then, leaning in, smiling, softer) So, uh... you married, Mel?

VANESSA (2)

(From FORGETTING TO FORGIVE by Glenn Alterman)
(Dramatic)
(50's to 70's)
(1 minute 12 seconds) All venues
(Vanessa tells her son why she tried to commit suicide)

I was watching Jay Leno last night! Yeah, Leno, I like a good laugh. But I didn't laugh, not last night. Didn't find him funny. Suddenly I realized, realized how alone I am here. I'm all by myself, sitting in bed, watching TV. And suddenly, I don't know, I felt hopeless! Crazy, right?. Anyway, the pills were by my bed. So I got up, went to the bathroom, got some water, got back in bed, turned the volume on the TV up very loud, and took the pills. Not all of them, just what I thought would be enough. Think I thought... thought watching Jay with all those pills in me... Thought maybe I'd start to laugh again, like I use to, when your father was here. Me and him, we'd always laugh at Leno, remember? Just seeing his chin could make me smile. So last night I thought, okay, I'll just take the pills. I'll take 'em and --- die, laughing. So I swallowed some and... soon my stomach started to hurt, I didn't feel good. -I don't remember calling you. Have no idea even what I even said. Barely remember dialing. No, you don't dial phones anymore, do ya? You push buttons. I pushed the buttons, and that's all I remember. I'm glad you came over, glad I'm not dead. Was a dumb idea, I don't know what the hell I was thinking.

JEN

(Dramatic)
(30's to 40's)
(1 minute) All venues
(Jen is in a very unhappy relationship. Here she talks about the ways out)

I drew my own door, and then walked through it. And then I went crashing through a window. The window that you drew, and then we met halfway. And then of course, we fought, just like always. Like we do every day, every night. Fight, yell, and curse. Ya know, I can't remember loving you. Sometimes I look at you over there, sitting at your desk, in your *container*. And I know if I go near you the lid will explode and I'll be forced out of the room.

I can't remember where we were when we even *liked* each other. How many lifetimes ago was that? Now ... I wonder who hates who more. And who will leave first? Who'll be the first to draw the door, grab the exit sign and leave?

You've worked very hard to convince me that you're the better person. It seemed to be so important to you. Okay then, be better. Draw the door and leave. Do it before I draw a window and jump out. And then you'll watch me as I fly away. Unless... you leave first. Why don't you? Please... just go.

WENDY

(Dramatic)
(30's to 50's)
(1 minute, 55 seconds) All venues, Agent's office
(After seeing a woman who might be dead or just sleeping, she decided to take action)

It was... a strange turn of events. 'Mean she was just sitting there, alone. Shopping bags, pocketbook, looked like anyone else. The Starbucks over on Forty-Second near Eighth. I'd just taken a break from job hunting, was exhausted. Ordered a coffee; was waiting, sitting, and saw her. But something seemed wrong. Think it was her head, it was like tilted. She was sitting there in that chair, eyes closed, her head kind of hanging. She looked dead. And everyone was just walking by, oblivious. New York, typical, right? People here can be...! Soon I noticed some saliva dripping out of her mouth. Large drops, dripping. Thought maybe she's just sleeping, tired from a long day of shopping. I moved a little closer. Was then I noticed her skin, it was pale, *yellow.* I decided she was definitely dead. (A beat) Her name was Alison Courter. Lives on East 52nd Street, or- lived. Had a husband, couple of kids. Hard to tell how old they were from the photographs. (Timidly) I... took her pocketbook. Well she didn't need it anymore! She had four hundred and ninety dollars in that wallet, and two credit cards; Amex and MasterCard. I used the MasterCard. Bought all the stuff we've needed. Drug store, hardware, groceries. I went on an all out buying spree, and it felt so good! I am so tired of always being broke! Living hand to mouth. Everyday day job hunting, unemployment's running out. This was a reprieve! It was an opportunity-- and I TOOK IT! (Then, softly) She was dead, what's the difference? (A beat) Do you ...think I'm heartless?

SHE (2)

(From The KINDNESS OF ENEMIES by Glenn Alterman)
(Serio-comedic)
(Adult- any age)
(1 minute, 23 seconds) All venues
(SHE hasn't recently gone home with HE, after meeting him at happy hour in bar. Here, she tells him why she won't give him her phone number)

Well you know how these things go. I'd give you my phone number and you probably wouldn't call (A slight edge) Well actually I wouldn't want you too. Wanna know why? Wouldn't be happy hour anymore. No more two for ones. Be just be a regular day, without magic or alcohol or anything. And if you did call, it would be like getting a call from a telemarketer. Someone I really don't know. Some somebody that just wants something from me. Something I wouldn't want to give them. But at least I know who they are, they're telemarketers. As opposed to you, who, well, the only thing I really know anything about, is you're allergic to dogs. And that's just sad. It is. That I know nothing about you. And you know nothing about me. So-- let's call it a night. Happy hour's over and I should get going.

See I really do have a home. Actually I have a very nice home, with pillows and soft lighting and plants, and worn Persian rugs. There's warmth everywhere in my home. But every now and then, get's a little cold there, like it did today. So I put on my coat and shoes and went out, to that bar, to warm up-- with someone, a stranger who I hoped might become a friend. Someone to share a happy hour with. But like everything else, happy hour's end. And, well, I have to go.

KAREN

(Serio-comedic)
(40's to 60's)
(55 seconds) All venues
(Karen is a hysteric. Here she is completely terrified over something, trying to get her husband to help)

Kidding? No, I'm not. I am absolutely not- kidding! This is real, our worst nightmare! We cannot, I MEAN, CANNOT...! I just called Eddie, Fran, everyone! And they all agreed, every single one of them! If they'd only stayed on the phone a little longer I could have gotten more into detail... But they were busy, had to hang up. But now everyone knows! S'probably even on the news. Look, I'm TRYING NOT TO PANIC! Trying to keep my feet on the ground, remain level headed. We must-stay—calm! (A beat) Now just tell me what to do, who should we call next? I mean it's probably too late, the damage is done, but... This isn't like the other times; it's not. Those were.... This time it's real! --Well are you just going to stand there and stare at me?! Call the police, F.B.I. DO SOMETHING! Why...?! Why are you just STARING?!

LITTLE LISA

(Dramatic)
(A young girl)
(1 minute, 45 seconds) All venues
(Little Lisa dreamt she saw her mother in heaven)

I dreamt... dreamt I was in a hotel-- but it was heaven. HEAVEN, yeah. And the room was so big. And it was white and wide and clean. Clean, real clean, yeah! Not a rat or a roach anywhere. And I'm sittin' on this big bed, and ya know what I did? Started rolling all over it, went from one side to the other. It smelled so fresh, like perfume. White sheets, warm covers, and big pillows! Then I got up, went to the door, opened it and looked out into the hall. Was the biggest hallway I ever saw! Like MILES long. And all white! With hundreds of rooms everywhere! So I started to walk down the hall, to look, to see. And I saw someone way down at the other end of the hall. And so I waved. And know what, they waved back, yeah! And then they started coming towards me. Running, faster! Got closer, closer! Was then I realized, (softly) that it was momma. MOMMA, YEAH! And she was ALIVE! And (softly, touched) she looked so pretty, yeah. Like when were kids. And momma came over to me and hugged me. She looked so healthy. Not strung out, not high, HEALTHY! And we hugged, me and momma. Felt so good. Then momma said "I miss you, girl." And I said, "I miss you too momma." And we just held each other like that, hugged. And then, well, then I woke up, was here, in my bed. Was dark outside, you were still sleeping. Room was real dark. And momma was gone; she was gone.

CEIL

(Dramatic)
(50's to 70's)
(1 minute 7 seconds) All venues
(Ceil talks about visiting her grandson and her husband)

I get such great joy out of feeding him, my grandson. He's such an innocent, so filled with life; I just love him. And I can tell just by the look in his eyes that he knows how much grandma loves him. As I hold his bottle and he drinks from it, those tiny hands touching mine. I'll tell ya, you live for moments like this. Time stands still.

(A beat) And then... later that day, or maybe another day, I visit Harry-- in the home. But Harry, he doesn't recognize me anymore. Well not that I can tell. And I sit there and tell him stories about the times we use to have. Times we all laughed, when the kids were growing up. I remember, and I tell him to remind him. (A beat) And I feed him, even though doesn't know who I am. And I sit there talking about old times. He opens his mouth and I feed him; very slowly. And sometimes his hand touches mine, for just a moment. And I look at him and I remember those dinners we all use to have in the kitchen, or those picnics in the park with the kids. I remember. (Smiling) When we all laughed, yeah, laughed, --and ate like pigs.

Chapter 6

Men's Monologues

JAKE

(From INSIDE by Glenn Alterman)
(Dramatic)
(50's to late 60s)
(2 minutes) All venues
(Jake tells another actor on a movie set how the AIDS epidemic affected his life)

Was just the luck of the draw! I wasn't wronged in any way, like you, John. Was just chance, luck; bad luck. And now much better people than me are gone. People who didn't deserve to die. Close friends. Lovers. People who mattered to me. Was AIDS, John. When it killed. When men died every day. Gay men- like me. --A plague was on our house. And it slew... eviscerated most of my friends, my lovers. Every day, another death. And between the constant worrying, "Am I next?" and the many memorials, I became terrified. Began to run, hide, pray. Every day another death. And I kept running, John, --till I found myself inside a shell. A place where I could hide, protect myself from everything outside, "out there." And I looked out from inside my shell and I saw the sky falling. And I stayed in there for a long time, years. Waiting for the rain to stop. ---Sure, I did things. Went to work, saw people, dinners. But I was never *really there*. I was living in constant fear. A bruise. A rash. A cough. Anything could.... So I stayed inside my shell waiting to weather the storm. *Pretending* I was alive. Doing things that living people did. And life went on. Years. You just continue.

So that's how I started doing this extra work on movies. Seemed like the perfect job. You just have to be a face in the crowd, just move along with the others.

Anyway, one day, there seemed to be a clearance; some sense that the worst had passed. I'd dodged the bullet, I was still alive. And the tide went back out to sea. And there were just bodies on the beach. Memories of men I once knew. Of a life I once lived.

You see, my bitterness doesn't come from trying not to remember John, like you. Mine comes from not being able to forget.

JACOB

(Serio-comedic)
(Adult- any age)
(1 minute, 21 seconds) All venues
(Jacob shares a terrifying experience he had right after he was born)

(Apprehensive) This man; black coat, black hat, --and he's coming towards me. And everyone there seemed to be having a really good time. 'Cept for me and this guy, this *mean man*. Well he seemed mean, Mike. You got to remember, I was very young. But I knew. Don't know how; but I did.

Anyway, it was like a party. Festive. Everyone there smiling, laughing- 'cept for me and this mean guy. And he's coming towards me, Mike, with a look of such *determination*. Was then I noticed, he was holding *a knife!* Well, some kind of cutting tool. And this guy, he had like a long white beard. He'd obviously just eaten. 'Cause there was like stuff stuck in his beard. These tiny bits of bagel. And people were yelling MOZEL TOV! MOZEL TOV! As he came closer and closer! And then he looked down at me. And I looked up at him. It was a moment, Mike, a moment of reckoning! Somehow I knew that after this, after this moment, my life would be forever changed. And I looked right into his eyes. I was what, maybe eight days old. I couldn't talk or yell, but something, something in me knew. Something in me wanted to scream, "PLEASE, MISTER, DON'T! I'm just a little baby. DON'T-DO-IT! DON'T! (A beat, softly, resigned) But. He. Did. He did it. After, there was a little bit of wine-- and again everyone yelled MAZEL TOV! (Succumbed) ---And that, well, that- was that.

STEVE

(Comedy)
(Mid twenties to early 40s)
(1 minute, 50 seconds) All venues.
(Steve tries to pick up a woman at Happy Hour at a bar)

Had my eye on the prize and she looked yum-yum good. Was hoping to get some *take out,* and there she was, next seat at the bar. We had drinks. Did some chit-chat, made some small talk. I held myself, erect. Time to make my move. I whispered, "How 'bout one more drink, baby. One more for the road less traveled." She smiled a come and get it kind of smile. Time to stop circling and zero in. She was game, I could tell, I was ready. Play time! So I downed my third or fourth drink, gently touched her hip with my hand. Just a brush by, not a full feel. She quickly sat up. And I said, "So, wanna go?" And I'm thinking how long will it take to get a cab? How long till I could get her back to my place My hand started circling her hip, slowly, caressing the curve. Nice. Tight. Firm.

"Touching." she said. She liked it, I could tell. But then quickly she repeated, (angrily) "TOUCHING!" But there was this look in her eye. Or maybe it was the tone in her voice. Suddenly everything came to screeching halt. "GET YOUR HAND OFF OF ME!" Was this a game, was she just playing? But the look in her eyes, ice water, cold snow. "No!" She repeated, "NO!" And the drawbridge fell down! And I stumbled back into my seat. Suddenly I was sober. (A childish whisper) "You mean "no" as in….? She stood up, said, GET YOUR GOD DAMNED HAND OFF OF ME! My hand fell limp, everything went limp. There would be no taxi ride, no take out. She suddenly seemed so tall. I became a little boy with his mommy. And mommy was angry. As she walked off she said, "Thanks for the drink." "What I do, what I do wrong? " She turned, left, was gone. I slumped back into my chair and ordered one more drink; one more for the road less traveled.

JOHN

(From TRESPASSED by Glenn Alterman)
(Dramatic)
(30's to 40's)
(1 minute 17 seconds) All venues
(John tells his friend Tom how his sister protected him from their physically abusive parents)

We all need help, sooner or later, now and then. Especially on any given night, when it's dark and late and the spirits are a flowin'. But me, I've had it with help. If anything Tom, in my life, I've been *over-helped*. And one thing you learn after a lifetime of being helped by someone, is that all help, all caring, comes with a cost. How too much help can sometimes be hurtful. Lily, my sister, she use to help. Yeah, she was a bona fide *comforter.* When we were kids, when the shit would hit the fan, when our parents would beat us with belts, Lily was right there to rescue me. Save me from their belts with buckles, from the hangers, or whatever was handy. Took some of the tension out of their day I guess. Couple of drinks and it was "Let's get the kids!" They'd work as a team, sort of a hunting party. And we'd hide, Lily and me, terrified. We'd hide while the missiles were blaring. As our drunk parents, foaming at the mouth, would frantically search for their little lost lambs for a little night's slaughter. As Lily and I hid under blankets or in boxes, far away from the fray. We were like Hansel nd Gretel, clinging, hiding.

BARRY

(From NOBODY'S FLOOD by Glenn Alterman)
(Dramatic)
(30's to 40's)
(1 minute 30 seconds) All venues
(Barry tells his parents about the last time he saw his brother)

Reason I came here that night was that Mickey had called me, said he needed me. Said he was determined to... So I came over to try... We argued, I yelled. He just wanted one thing to go down to the ocean with me. Said he was too weak to get there by himself, that he needed my help. I kept saying no, but finally I agreed.

He told me it'd become like a war zone with you two, and he was the battlefield. He couldn't take it anymore. And you know how he loved the water, the beach. He threatened to crawl down there if he had too. And so finally, as usual, I gave in. I just wanted him to have some dignity, ma. So I carried him down to the beach.

We sat there, had like a little party, talked about old times, even told a few jokes, some laughs. But then... he got like real quiet. We just sat there in the dark, listening to the ocean. He drank some vodka, took the pills. I just sat there, watched. Then he hugged me, said, "I love you Barry." I told him I loved him too, always would. Then he stood up, and, I don't know how, but he slowly walked down to the water.

I got up, followed him, still hoping he'd change his mind. Then I watched him go in, swim out till ... I couldn't see him anymore. Till he just like disappeared. I stood there at the water for a while, watching the waves come in. Still hoping... Then I left, went to the airport, waited for Brenda.

HERMAN

(Dramatic)
(25 to 45)
(2 minutes 27 seconds) Agent's office, longer auditions, classroom work
(After leaving a Lot Less bargain store, Herman sees a man lying on the sidewalk looking very pale)

Okay, so I'm just leaving the Lot Less discount store on West 47th Street. And I'm feeling great. According to my receipt I just saved over forty bucks! Anyway, I walk out and notice this guy on the ground. At first I thought, okay, another drunk, you know, New York. But then I notice, he's well dressed; jacket, tie, overcoat. Middle aged, Asian guy, wearing glasses, and VERY PALE. This was no drunk. Soon a crowd starts gathering, staring. Everyone asking, "S'he okay?" But none of them doing a thing, just staring! So I bend down, ask the guy if he's alright. But he was really out of it. His breathing was really heavy and the only thing moving was his hand, his right hand. It was like shaking, clinging tightly to his I-phone.

I call 911! Soon more people are gathering, NOBODY DOING A DAMN THING, just staring! Anyway, the 911 operator asks where's my emergency. I looked up, saw the number on the door to the store, gave it to her. Told her, "Tell the cops to hurry, there's a guy really out of it, looks really bad." Again she asks me the address! Again I gave it to her! TELL THEM TO HURRY, SEND AN AMBULANCE!

I bend down, tell him helps on the way. He tries to sit up, but collapses back down, "Please, mister, just lie down, s'gonna be okay." He's sweating, had peed himself, was even more pale. So I think this guy's gonna DIE.

FINALLY the cops come. I tell 'em I'm the one who called. This woman cop bends down, tries talking to the guy, then gets on her walkie-talkie, calls for an ambulance. Crowds getting larger. Few minutes later, the ambulance shows up. The woman cop turns to me, says, "Thank you for calling, we got this." "Oh, okay." I say. Shows over everyone on your way.

The guys from the ambulance rush over, lift the guy up, take him away. I stand there in front of the store with my shopping bag, just shaking. I mean I really didn't know him but....

So I start walking down 47th Street, heading home, thinking What the hell was that about?! And I realize that suddenly my bag full of Lot Less bargains seem so, I don't know, unimportant. All I could think was I hope that guys okay, hope he makes it.

LOUIS

(Comedic)
(30's to 50's)
(1 minute, 15 seconds) All venues
(Louis' erotic moment with a woman sitting in a chair)

(Passionately) I love you! I. LOVE. YOU! Everything-about-you! Your face; your body! Since the minute I first saw you! You know what I'd love to do right now?! I'd love to GRAB you, pull you right out of that chair, hold you in my arms, and kiss every inch of you! And then I'd whisk you away. Take you--- to the south of France. A beach. A hot beach with white sand. Nice would be nice. Or we could go to Cannes.

And we'd just drink wine, naked, alone. The TWO OF US, an empty beach, baking in a hot sun. Our skin, burning! Our bodies—on fire! Just you and me lusting...! Making love; MAKING -LOVE!

(HE suddenly stops, pulls his stomach in, stands tall, looks at her, but now with just a slight smile His voice changes, becomes softer, more "professional.")

So... did you happen to see anything you liked on the menu? ...Hm. No? (Slight professional smile) May I suggest the house specialty? It's quite good tonight, exceptional. Made to order. (Slowly, softly, professional) Our Chef Jean's Coq Au Vin. It's made with delicious skin on, chicken thighs, large button mushrooms, bacon, and butter. (His voice slowly fades as he smiles friendly but professional) Cooked to taste in a delicious red wine, with just... just - a touch of thyme. I believe... I think you might really enjoy it. I think you really would.

CARL

(Serio-comedic)
(Teenager)
(1 minute) All venues
(Carl confronts his little brother about money he stole from their mother)

She found out, she knows the money's missing. Mom-*knows!* And it hadda be you! And if you don't admit it, I swear, I'm going to go in there right now, and tell her. I am not getting a beating 'cause of you. You stole it, why should I have to pay? Just go in there and say "Ma, it was me, I stole ya money, I'm really, really sorry." What'll she do, yell at you? Big deal.

...Well what are you waiting for? Don't just sit there and stare at me! Look, I know it was you. And I even know why. You saw my new sneakers and you wanted a pair too. Motive, you had a motive. You were jealous, like always.

Look, if you go in there and admit it, I'll let you wear my sneakers, okay? 'Sides you know she won't hit you, never does. S'just me, *I'm* her punching bag. ` Anytime something goes wrong I get the belt, the beating. Now just go ahead, go ahead, go in there! Just tell her you took it and you're really sorry. What are you waiting for? GO!

HE

(FROM BENCHMARKS Glenn Alterman)
(Dramatic)
(30's to 60's)
(1 minute, 17 seconds) All venues
(HE has just met Telly at a bus stop and they discuss waiting for the bus).

You know those people you were just talking about, the one's who were forced to sit on the benches, the commoners? I bet you some of them weren't all that unhappy. I mean think about it, they did have a place to sit; to rest. Maybe some of them were actually even content. Thought, "You know, could be worse. I could be sitting on the floor, the ground, in the dirt." I think what I'm trying to say Telly, is that maybe sometimes cushiony chairs don't always make for comfortable seating. There's no guarantee. Sometimes just making do, being content with where you happen to be seated can be enough. (Smiling) Telly, I really don't know you very well. And excuse me for being so forward. But it's my guess you've been sitting here on this bench, waiting for a bus, for quite a while. And I have a feeling a couple of buses may have come and gone and you didn't get on them. Maybe you're one of those people you were talking about. The ones who hated sitting on benches, but they did. They just sat and sat, and remained unhappy. And then blamed it on the bench. Maybe it's time, Telly. To get up, get on the bus, and go.

There's nothing here, just some wood and cement; a bench on a highway. But you'll never get there if you remain here. It's a bus stop. It's supposed to be temporary; a waiting point. Somewhere between here and where you want to go. ...So, what do you say?

TED

(From TIME WOUNDS ALL HEELS by Glenn Alterman)
(Dramatic)
(55 seconds) All venues
(Ted advises his young business partner to settle down in life rather than playing the field)

I'm a very lucky man. And don't think I take it for granted, I count my blessings. I must have done something REALY RIGHT in one of my past lives. And my wife, Nancy, you know her, she's my reward. And let me tell ya Tom, that woman's there for me, hand and foot. And me, I'd kill for her. Loyalty; it's not just a word. Just talking about her (Patting his chest) gives me like a pain, right here in my chest! (Hitting his chest, harder) Right here, yeah! You have no idea. Pain! Sharp! Caring! "All You Need Is Love", Tom. And I hope someday you'll get to experience this same feeling. I hope you meet that certain someone who will give your life meaning. I wish that for you, because I care about you, you're my partner, my friend. .But the way you're living your life now, bouncing from bed to bed, broad to broad; meaningless! Not that I mean to judge. S'just I care about you- like a son. Whatiya say?

NICKY

(Comedy)
(Adult- any age)
(1 minute) All venues
(Nicky is obsessed with the sound of his own voice.)

I like to talk. Actually, I like to hear myself talk. Come on, I've got a great voice, right? In restaurants, people turn, look, all the time. They admire the sound, the quality. I pretend not to notice, you know, but I do. I'll talk louder to the person I'm talking too. Sometimes, sometimes I purposely strike up a conversation with a person at the next table. Talk to them about anything, doesn't matter, just so people can hear me. And in a crowded elevator, people always move aside, just to get a better view of the guy with the voice, talking on his phone. (Smiling) Actually, sometimes I'm not really talking to anyone at all; I just pretend I'm on the phone. (A smile) And sometimes, at home, I talk to myself in the mirror. (Doing a DeNiro) "You talking; to me? You talkin' to me? Well I'm the only one here." See when I do that, I get to see what everyone else gets to hear, when they're treated to the pleasure of my most incredible voice.

CHARLIE

(Dramatic)
(30 to 40)
(1 minute) All venues
(Charlie has spent the last five years in prison. Here he tells his wife what it's like being home again)

I don't know what to say. S'kina hard to make small talk now, you know? (A beat) I gotta ask, why'd you stop coming, huh? You give up on me? (A beat) S'matter, cat got your tongue? Even though I told you, I SWORE I was innocent! And you said you believed me. But if you believed me, then why'd you stop coming? Prison's a very lonely place. I kept holding on to the belief that you believed me. But- when you stopped coming and stopped accepting my phone calls... Why?

Well, I'm sorry, but no, there won't be any divorce. I waited five long years to come home and now I'm here. Thank God for the DNA, huh honey? Aren't you happy? I'm back in the house. The house that I paid for--- and I am not leaving. ...Now, why don't you go get the kids, I want to say hello. Go ahead, tell them daddy's home. I can't wait to see the look on their faces.

RONALD

(Dramatic)
(30's to 40's)
(1 minute 30 seconds) All venues
(Another night and Ronald has insomnia. Something haunts him and he can't stop thinking about it)

I dreamt I was dreaming, but then I woke up. Was about 3 A.M. and I realized I had been sleeping after all. So I sat up and thought, "Okay, 3 A.M. now what?" Here we go again. So I got out of bed, turned on the T.V., tried to read a book, fed the cat, then got back in bed and rolled around restlessly. So I went over to the window, looked out. And thought about her. Wondered where she was, what she was doing. Wondered if she was happy, if she had had her first love yet.

Then- I thought about my ex-wife. It's funny how some anger never goes away. It attaches itself to you. I wondered if she was satisfied with what she did to me, us. Wondered if she had trouble sleeping at night.

Then I remembered all the days, the searches, the disappointments. The hope that some day I'd find her. No matter where my wife took her I'd find her. People don't just disappear, fathers don't give up! Crimes don't go unpunished.

Then I thought about the last time I saw her, just a baby in a crib. And my holding her, then sitting there watching her sleep. If only I could just hold her one more time! Where is she? Where?!

MARK

(Comedy)
(30 to 50)
(1 minute 25 seconds) All venues
(Mark has brought home a co-worker and they've just had sex.)

(Sweet, a bit meek) That was... incredible. Really. It's funny, y'know, you think you know someone, right? 'Mean we talk every day at work, so polite, business-like. I had no idea, (playful) you are one hot lady! (Sincerely) I'll be honest with you, I had some considerations about bringing you back tonight. I know, crazy. But I hardly ever invite anyone back here. And then there's that thing about shitting where you eat. Y'know, same office, next cubicle, all these years. But I felt we kind of really know each other, was worth the risk.

And when you shared all that stuff last week about being burned by all those guys you went home with, those creeps, really broke my heart. S'when I realized I really care about you. That you're not just a co-worker in the next cubicle, not anymore. I know, I'm talking too much, I'll stop. But you're always saying, "Mark, you should open up, let people see who you really are." Well I am, and you're right, and this feels really good! I'm no longer that turtle in a shell. I'M OPEN ALICE, OPEN! THIS IS WHO I AM! THIS IS ME! And now that we've had sex and really know each other we should.... Hey, where you going? S'early. ... Are you leaving?! (Then calling to her, sadly) What's the matter? ... Alice...? (Then, angrily) Alice... Alice, I'm talking to you, come back here!

MEL

(From DITMAS by Glenn Alterman)
(Dramatic)
(30's to 50's)
(1 minute 20 seconds) All venues
(Mel meets a former roommate in a bar and tells her how much he's changed since their days at school.)

Sharon, we know each other. And not from this bar or this neighborhood. We knew each other years ago, when we both went to Ditmas; Ditmas Junior High. We were in the same grade, took some of the same classes. Anyway, you were always very kind to me. The other kids were always making fun of me, bullying me. Made my life a real hell. (Softly) But, see, well, I was different back then. Sharon, I wasn't "Mel" then. I was—"Marla." Marla, yeah. Skinny, pimply Marla. Wore those thick, dark glasses, which the other kids always loved knocking off my face. I was a real mess. Had no idea who I really was. But you were always so kind to me, protected me. Told the other kids they better leave me alone- or else! And they knew you meant it, you were pretty tough. Couple of times you even took me by the hand to my next class. You were like my personal bodyguard, my guardian angel. You took care of me Sharon, and I'll never forget it. And I just… just want to say thank you.

HERB

(From IN THE BAG by Glenn Alterman)
(Serio-comedic)
(40's to 50's)
(1 minute, 42 seconds) All venues
(Herb talks about how a patient who came onto him while in drag)

Drag, full drag, yeah! Little yellow dress, dainty hat. And he just sat there, *pretending* it was a typical session. So I just *stared,* waited to see what he had to say. The way he looked at me, Mark like *sexual, seductive*. I mean I could tell; he *wanted* me. Totally inappropriate!

Then he sat forward in the chair, and said, (Seductively) "C'mon, you know this is what you want. Who we kidding here, Herbie?" Yeah, called me Herbie. Not Doctor Klenner, HERBIE! Then he said, "You want some of this HERBIE?"

I mean Mark, you have to understand. This guy, he's so *masculine.* Well built, drives a truck; listens to country music for Christ's sake! A real redneck, Republican! Then he opens his legs--- and I notice he's wearing like little lace *pink* panties! Mark, he's married, has like 5 kids, goes to church every week. Devout Christian!

Then... he starts moving in on me, yeah, till he's practically on top of me. And HE'S A BIG GUY! Reminds of that actor, what's his name?Joe Manganiello!

So finally I just said, "Sit back in your chair, this is TOTALLY INAPPROPRIATE! ---Didn't stop him though, kept moving towards me. Could feel his face getting closer. His *breath.* And his tongue, it was dripping, reminded me of that movie *Alien.* You know, with that thing that pops out, that tongue... And he s coming closer and closer! CLOSER and CLOSER! ---And then, well, then I woke up. Woke up and was shaking; terrified. And the worst part, I have a session with him today, two o'clock! I don't know if I'll even able to look him in the eyes. 'Mean those pink panties, that yellow dress, that TONGUE!

(A beat, exhausted) C'mere, Mark, please, come back to bed, just for a minute. I'm a mess. Look at me, I'm still shaking. Give me a hug before you go to work. C'mon, please, I need a hug.

SEBASTIAN

(From THE LAST KEY by Glenn Alterman)
(Dramatic)
(30's to 40's)
(1 minute, 22 seconds) All venues
(Sebastian tells Skipper how he ended up in Key West)

Well, to make a long story short, I was doing some traveling with my cousin, Catherine. Beautiful woman, Catherine. Men just flocked to her, everywhere we went. Was summer; a burning hot day. And we were in this town called Cabeza de Lobo. Charming place. Lots of very young attractive men, my cup of tea. I was there *shopping* you might say. And Catherine was being very helpful. And they all seemed very friendly in Cabeza de Lobo; at first. Inviting, welcoming. Pick and chose time. But as sometimes happens, things don't always go quite as planned. The tide changed most dramatically. An incident, an occurrence near a beach. A beach Catherine and I had frequented several times before. We were well known there by the locals. But there were these young thugs, you see, with ugly thoughts and very sharp weapons. Soon a chase ensued. Things turned mean, quickly, terrifying! We ran, *fled* like our lives depended on it! See, they didn't just want money, these men, they wanted more. We were prey, and they were hunters. And suddenly... suddenly they caught up to me, I was captured and I gave up. There was violence, an attack, and I left; abruptly. I left Cabeza de Lobo and ended up here in Key West.

TED (2)

(From THE KINDNESS OF ENEMIES by Glenn Alterman)
(Dramatic)
(50's to 70's)
(1 minute) All venues
(Ted tells his business partner what he discovered on some security cameras he recently installed in his home)

Did I happen to tell you I had security cameras installed throughout my house? Was gonna be my little anniversary gift to my Nancy; surprise. And you know what I've learned? That sometimes there are things going on right under your nose that you had no idea of. Those cameras are state of the art. Any motion, any motion at all, and... So I guess when I was away yesterday there was some motion in my house. Judging by that video I'd say there was there was a lot of motion. A lot of motion and emotion; a lot of activity. And I learned something, about my wife. About my wife and you, my business partner. My partner, who I've always treated like a son. You and my wife--- in my bedroom! YOU- and MY WIFE! Both of you saying all kinds of things, some of them very naughty. Y'know, Nancy never said anything like that to me, ever. Guess what I'm trying to say is--- I know; I know.

SON

(From FORGETTING TO FORGIVE by Glenn Alterman)
(Dramatic)
(Late 40's to late 50)
(1 minute, 23 seconds) All venues
(SON realizes that he and his mother have had a similar experience with men in their lives)

I understand, ma. I do. And I feel the same way, yeah. There's an early expiration date for *older men* in the gay scene, and I passed it a while ago. The first sign of gray and you become *invisible*. Now I'm considered a "daddy" or "granddaddy," I don't know. And- Michael left me, yeah, a few weeks ago. Found himself a younger model. Really caught me off guard, it did. I mean this was the man I loved! We'd been through so much together, so many years. Those summers on Fire Island, then setting up a home, a life, friends, travel. And then when the tides turned, AIDS, losing friends. We clung to each other like frightened kids. We were terrified, but we were *together.*

And then when things started to ease up with Aids, we realized we didn't have to cling so tight anymore. Guess that's when we started to let go. We didn't need each other so much.

Oh I knew he was cheating. Kept hoping it would pass. After he left it got very bad. I actually thought about ending it. I didn't want to live anymore, ma. So one night I went up on my roof, stood there and decided I was going to jump. But I didn't do it, you know why? Because of you, ma. I thought who'd take care of you if you need anything. (Smiling) Who'd bring you your bagels on Sunday mornings? So in a way you could say, you saved me. (Suddenly playfully) Guess what I'm saying, ma, is we both lost our men, but, hell, we're still at the dance.

MR. ANONYMOUS

(Dramatic)
(Adult, any age)
(1 minute, 20 seconds) All venues
(Mr. Anonymous, a gentle man with an indistinguishable face talks about his secret life.)

Little secrets, private joys. Goes back I guess to when I was just an altar boy. Snuck into the church late one night when no one was there. Then I secretly filled the contribution box with every penny I'd earned that year. Then the next day, as they scratched their heads, trying to figure out where all that money come from, I just stood there, not saying anything. (a playful smile) My secret was born, "Mr. Anonymous."

Then, over the years, Mr. A really took flight. Saving folks from fires, stopping muggings, rapes, bringing crash victims to hospital emergency rooms, and then always, I'd silently disappear. The victims wondering, was it a dream? "Who was he?"

See, I've got the perfect face for this kind of thing. I blend, merge. My disguise is my sameness. I love the chaos that ensues, people wondering who I was and where I went. Why ruin my fun with fame? I love my life of the rescuing peek-a-boo without a thank you.

See, my face is my fortune, my sameness, my pride. I just want to be a shadow, a no-one, just another guy. I just wish to remain (a soft smile) Mr. Anonymous.

RANDY

(From THE VIEW by Glenn Alterman)
(Serio-comedic)
(20's to 30's)
(55 seconds) All venues
(Randy tells a mountain ranger about the last time he saw his brother-in-law)

To be honest, I don't really care for my brother-in-law. Was almost like a reprieve, a breather when we got separated. Truth be told, I actually hate him. And I hated the idea that I even had to spend time with him. I only agreed because my sister insisted. She can be very… Anyway he'd been complaining all day. He's one of those people who actually gets off on complaining. Nothing's good enough for him. Probably feels that way about my sister too. Maybe that's why they don't have kids or pets or anything. When I think about it they're perfect for each other. Anyway, we'd been hiking up the mountain, found these trails, roads going in all different directions. And somehow, I don't know, somehow, we got separated. Yeah, sure, I'm glad we did, I'd had enough of him. But—I certainly didn't push him off that cliff. Must have been an accident, I'm sure he just fell. So, you'll have to ask my sister what actually happened I wasn't there. Or- you can ask him if he ever comes out of that coma.

STAN

(Dramatic)
(30's to 50)
(1 minute 6 seconds) All venues
(Stan has been caught with an under age girl. Here, he tries to explain to his wife what happened)

She said... told me she was nineteen. Nineteen, that's what she said. She looked much older. It was dark, I had no idea she.... I know, I know, that doesn't really matter. But honey, you have to... There's something about being alone in a hotel, far from home. You get so lonely, so damn... Missing you, the kids. So I had a couple of drinks. It was late, I couldn't call, and I couldn't sleep. Maybe I was a little drunk, I don't know. So I decided to take a ride. I know, stupid idea. So I'm driving and I saw her on the road and stopped. She said she needed a lift. We talked. I asked her age. She lied. She got in, we started driving. We just talked. But soon the conversation got I don't know, sexual. And I got turned on. Told you, I was a little drunk. Next thing I knew the cops came. And now this nightmare. Look, I was wrong, I know. But I need you. They want to put me away. Honey it was a lapse in judgment. The drinks, lonely. I never... ... Baby, try to understand. Was a one-time thing.

ROB

(Dramatic)
(30's to 40's)
(1 minute 4 seconds) All venues
(Rob's son had committed a horrific crime. Here he tries to apologize to someone who was related to a victim)

Kevin's a good kid, well, he was. I just wasn't a very good father I guess. Anyway you don't want to hear about any of that. I just need you to know I cared about him. But the courts... They felt I was unfit. So they took him away. Best I could do was sneak a phone call to him now and then, or see him going to school, parked in my car. I thought my wife had everything under control, that's what she told me, "Everything's fine, he's doing well." But then I found out he was having problems. But she denied it, said he was fine; she lied!

(A beat) I can't imagine what you're going through. I don't know if your meeting me today can help in any way. But thank you for seeing me. All the other parents refused to, just hung up. (A beat) Look, I don't know what else I can say other than I'm sorry. He was... Guess I should go. I don't think my being here's helping. I was hoping... It was an attempt.... I'm... so sorry.

GENE

(Serio-comedic)
(Mid-40's to 60)
(1 minute 30 seconds) All venues
(The countess, a drag queen has received a male escort as a birthday gift. Here he chats with the shy escort)

Give me some booze and I can even out-bitch Bette. Rum and Coke and I'm Joan Crawford, reincarnate. They don't call me the Countess for nothing. Do you even know who Bette Davis and Joan Crawford were? I thought not, can see it in your eyes. They were another lifetime ago, when I was almost as young as you. God, was I ever almost as young as you? Well sweets, you're a captive audience tonight. You know, you really are quite the looker. Tommy's got good taste, I must thank him. (Smiling) The Countess is pleased. Tommy told me you were very quiet, you are. But I kind of like that. This way I can do all the talking. And the Countess loves to talk as you can tell. Few little drinks and I can filibuster, baby, with the best of them. ...That was a little joke. Well, you're not here to have a meaningful conversation with me. Actually, I kind of hate meaningful conversations.

So- let the festivities begin! Guess we should first get undressed, huh? Bathrooms over there if you'd like to wash up. I'll just go into the bedroom, get myself ready. Give me a few minutes, huh?

Y'know, I always love the anticipation, the drama of waiting. But you mustn't keep the Countess waiting too long. Because then she might just fall asleep and miss the whole thing. And that would be a terrible shame, especially on my birthday.

SKIPPER

(From THE LAST KEY by Glenn Alterman)
(Dramatic)
(20's to 30's)
(55 seconds) All venues
(Skipper tells Sebastian how he ended up in Key West)

I had a friend; his name was Brick. We were very close, close as you can get I guess. Anyway, we played football together. Were team mates, me and Brick. He was my best-buddy. We'd go out drinking, have ourselves one hell of a time; tear up the town! We were inseparable! -But there was this woman, her name was Maggie and... long story short, it turned into a horrible mess. Wrong time, wrong place, wrong....

Broke my heart, my spirit. One night, one very warm, sad summer night I got myself drunk, shit-faced. And in some very dark moment I decided to... Well, that's how I ended up here.

JOHN

(From INSIDE by Glenn Alterman)
(Dramatic)
(Mid 30's to mid 50's)
(2 minutes 45 seconds) Agent's office, longer auditions, classroom work
(John explains to a man he's just met where he's been many years)

Small talk? Yeah, I'm an expert at it. --- You really want to know what it was like there? -Was like a nightmare. Every day, every minute, every year. Windows and walls. Staring. Lost in my head. See, I had... There was this window, small window with a view of —well, nothing. So I could never tell if it was sunny or cloudy outside. You see, my window faced these high brick walls. And so every day I'd just sit there in my cell with my thoughts- bouncing off those walls! Bing, bing, like ping pong balls bouncing! BING! BING! And I was filled with rage, resentment! I mean I had a right to be, right?

Anyway, every day we'd do the same thing. Wake up. Shower. Have some chow. Take a dump. Do our chores. Lift weights. Maybe play ball with some of the guys in the courtyard. Always being watched by them, the guards with their big guns. Fingers ready. And we'd all just sit there, shoot the shit. *Small talk*. About nothing. 'Cause nothing ever really happened. But when someone got released, *that* was big news!

And sometimes, in the nooks, some corner, maybe in the laundry room, some guy, a friend, someone I *thought* I knew, would make a mistake. He'd touch me. And I'd quickly remind him. Say, "Sorry, keep ya hands to yourself. I'm not your go to guy to for that. Find someone else." Then he'd walk away, and we'd never mention it. Was just the way it was there.

And the sun would go up and the sun would come down. But I'd never see the sun from my cell. I'd look out my window at that wall and think (Enraged) "WHY?! I'M INNOCENT, WHY AM I HERE!!"

(Calmer) Only hope I ever had was that my next appeals lawyer would have the key. Prove my case, set me free. And while waiting I WILLED MYSELF, Jacob, to forgive, not-be-bitter! But it was a battle. I FORCED MYSELF TO FORGIVE THEM!

And for fourteen years and eleven days...! (Then, suddenly, softer) Then one day it was rec-tif-ied. They found the guy. -D-N-A! And the door opened and I was set free. And they said they were sorry, and they gave me this brand-new-blue-suit.

And the door closed behind me. And I didn't look back. And my family was waiting. And we all cried, held each other.

And I went home and life went on. But I had to get a job. But then I had to explain where I'd been all those years. That they made a "mistake." But I learned most employers don't hire people with "mistakes" in their past. There's no forgiving.

(A beat) So- that's how I began doing extra work on movies. I was perfectly prepared. 'Mean we were taught very well in prison; just follow instructions. Walk when told, sit when told. Be seen and not heard. You're an extra. (Softly) Just. ---Say ---Nothing.

SEARS

(From TRESPASSED by Glenn Alterman)
(Serio-comedic)
(30's to 40's)
(1 minute 24 seconds) All venues
(Sears, a bad cop, prepares his married girlfriend for an upcoming investigation)

C'mon Lily, you can do this. They're just questions. I do this every day, know exactly what they'll ask. You just have to act like you know from nothing. Be simple, I swear, you'll see.

Okay, so they'll phone first. Tell 'em you just heard. You just have to act surprised, try to cry. Make sure they hear you crying. Tell 'em you're too upset to talk, that you have to hang up. Then pretty soon some detective will show up, ask you some questions. If you can, cry some more. Let the tears flow like Niagara. Use an onion if you have to. They'll try to calm you. Then they'll just look around for a while, then leave. Just like that, easy as pie.

Hey, they got no reason to suspect you. No one knew about your fights with him, that he abused you. Just remember, it was an accident! A fall, and that's all. Not a shove or push, nothing done on purpose. And when they find his body, it'll be obvious Hey, he was unhappy, a messed up drunk. And that'll be the end of it.

Then, you just have to wait to get the money. And when it's safe, after a few months, we'll meet up in Mexico. Marguerites by the pool, hired help by the handful. Postcards to all our friends, saying, "Having a wonderful time, wish you were here!" (A beat) Baby, I love you, you know that. Just want you to be happy. Now lets practice this one more time, you can do it.

ZACK

(From THE HIGH LOW LIFE by Glenn Alterman)
(Serio-comedic)
(25 to 30)
(1 minute 40 seconds) All venues
(Zack, a drug addict tells his girlfriend how he's going to be a famous writer)

I'm gonna write something today, baby. I will, you'll see! It'll be the story of you and me. And this book, this books gonna make me immortal! Everyone will know my name! Just wait and see! People will point to me on the street and say "Hey, there's that dude who wrote that book; THE BOOK!"

Soon little kids will sneak into libraries just to read the dirty parts. And their teachers will warn them, "Do-not-read-that-man's-book! They'll tell them it's too dirty! But little kids, especially little boys got a "willy" of their own. And so I will definitely include *extra porno passages* just for the boys and their big brothers. 'Cause I'm compassionate, I care. 'Cause I remember growin' up how hard it was to find good dirty parts in books. My never ending search to find those passages that could stimulate my young hormones, give me some rapid release.

And then soon the boys'll tell their friends, and their friends. And they might even meet in groups to read the dirty parts out loud. 'Cause little boys do that.

And then soon, the girl's, hearing about all the fun the boys are having, will want to read it too. And the girl's, they'll just love it! 'Cause they'll realize that at it's heart it's really a love story. And it is.

And then the kid's parents will hear about all the excitement about the book and will start buying it to find out what all the buzz is about. And they'll love it too, yeah! And what was once an underground sensation will become a New York Times best seller.

And it'll all be because of you, and the night at Snyders when you helped me home and took care of me. And I fell in love with you, and never left. All of it, it'll all be in the book. I love you, baby!

Overdone Monologues

This is just a short list based on casting directors/Agent's experiences at auditions. There are certainly many more. Tennessee Williams, Arthur Miller, Wendy Wasserstein, Theresa Rebeck, Neil Simon, Christopher Durang, John Guare, John Patrick Shanley, David Mamet, seem to be the playwrights with the most overused monologues.

Laughing Wild, 'Dentitiy Crisis – Christopher Durang
Angels in America–Tony Kushner
Five Women Wearing the Same Dress – Alan Ball
The Shadow Box – Michael Cristofer
Beyond Therapy – Christopher Durang (and most other Durang plays!)
The House of Blue Leaves – John Guare
Stop Kiss – Diana Son
Night Luster – Laura Harrington
Lobby Hero – Kenneth Lonergan
A Girl's Guide to Chaos – Cynthia Heimel
Painting Churches – Tina Howe
A...My Name is Alice – Joan Micklin Silver and Julianne Boyd
Brilliant Traces – Cindy Lou Johnson
Romantic Comedy – Bernard Slade
Reasons to be Pretty – Neil Labute (and most other Labute plays!)
Oleanna – David Mamet
Talking With – Jane Martin
Picasso at the Lapin Agile – Steve Martin
In the Boom Boom Room – David Rabe
Red Light Winter – Adam Rapp

Loose Knit – Theresa Rebeck
Spike Heels – Theresa Rebeck (most Rebeck plays!)
Dog Sees God – Burt V. Royal
I Hate Hamlet – Paul Rudnick
Danny and the Deep Blue Sea – John Patrick Shanley
Brighton Beach Memoirs – Neil Simon
Chapter Two – Neil Simon (and most other Simon plays!)
The Food Chain – Nicky Silver (and most other Silver plays!)
Nuts – Tom Topor
Uncommon Women and Others – Wendy Wasserstein
Getting Out – Marsha Norman
Cowboy Mouth – Sam Shepard
Blue Window – Craig Lucas
Crimes of the Heart- Beth Henley
The Woolgatherer and Extremities – William Mastrosimone

Permissions

Contact the following for performance rights:

Monologues from *After* by Glenn Alterman. Published in 2011 *The Best Ten Minute Plays For Two Or Three Actors* (Smith and Kraus) (contact: toryfran@gmail.com)

Monologues From *Nobody's Flood, Benchmarks, Phone, Forgetting to Forgive, Ditmas* by Glenn Alterman
Contact Arthur Rosen and Associates (Arthurrosen46@gmail.com)

For Monologues from *The High Low Life* by Glenn Alterman
Contact Mel Drucker Literary (Meldrucker@gmail.com)

Monologues from *Trespassed, The Kindness of Enemies, Inside, The Last Key, The View* by Glenn Alterman
Contact Fran Tory (toryfran@gmail.com)

Time Wounds All Heels by Glenn Alterman
Published in *The Best Ten-Minute Plays of 2016* (Smith and Kraus) Contact Fran Tory (toryfran@gmail.com.)

About The Author

Glenn Alterman is a multi award winning playwright, the author of twenty-nine theater related books (including nine books of original monologues), a screenwriter, and a highly respected monologue/audition acting coach.

Mr. Alterman received a 2017 French Arts Grant. Most recently he was a Jerry Kaufman Award Recipient. He was awarded the first Julio T. Nunez Artist's Grant, The Arts and Letters Award in Drama, the Bloomington Playwrights Project Award "Shiner Award" and has won over 60 playwriting awards, including being a five-time finalist at The Actor's Theater of Louisville Ten- Minute Play Competition.

He holds the world record for being "The Author of The Most Published Original Monologues For Actors" (RecordSetter.com and soon The Guinness Book of World Records).

His plays and monologues have appeared in over 50 Best Play, Best Short Play and Best Monologue anthologies.

His book, Writing *The Ten-Minute Play* (Applause Cinema and Theater Books), is now part of the curriculum of many college playwriting courses.

Mr. Alterman's plays, *Like Family* and *The Pecking Order,* were optioned by Red Eye Films (with Alterman writing the screenplay). His play, *Solace,* was produced off-Broadway by the Circle East Theater Company (formerly Circle Rep Theater Company).

Coulda-Woulda-Shoulda won the Three Genres Playwriting Competition- twice. The prize included ongoing publication of the play (along with plays by Edward Albee and William Inge) in the Prentice Hall textbook The Writing of Poetry, Prose and Drama. It is one of the most widely used writing textbooks in colleges today.

Mr. Alterman wrote the book for *Heartstrings: The National Tour* (commissioned by DIFFA, the Design Industries Foundation for Aids), a thirty-five city tour that starred Michelle Pfeiffer, Ron Silver, Susan Sarandon, Marlo Thomas, and others. Other plays include *Kiss Me When It's Over* (commissioned by E. Weissman Productions), starring and directed by André De Shields, *Tourists of the Mindfield* (finalist in the L. Arnold Weissberger Playwriting Competition at New Dramatists), and *Street Talk/Uptown* (based on his monologue books), produced at the West Coast Ensemble.

Mr. Alterman's work has been performed at Primary Stages, Ensemble Studio Theater (EST), Circle in the Square Downtown, HERE, LaMaMa, Circle Repertory Theater Company, at the Duplex, Playwrights Horizons, at several theaters on Theater Row in New York, as well as at many theaters around the country and on three continents.

www.Glennalterman.com
www.Glennaltermanplaywright.com